MOTOR BOATING

MOTOR BOATING

Alex McMullen

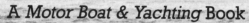

A Motor Boat & Yachting Book

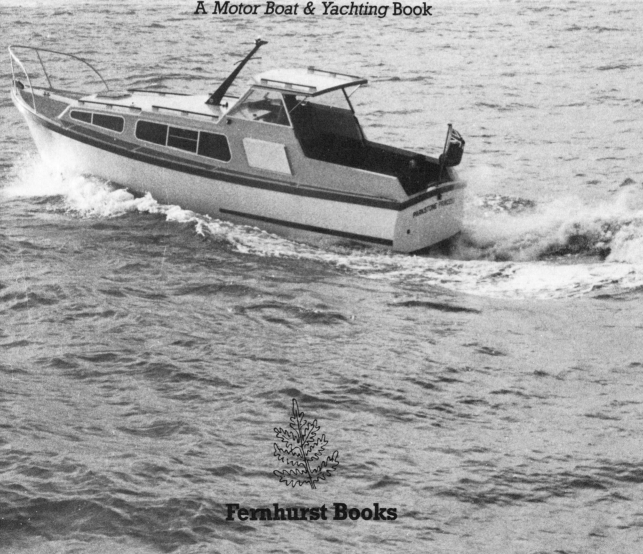

Fernhurst Books

First published 1988 by
Fernhurst Books, 31 Church Road, Hove, East Sussex

Printed and bound in Great Britain

British Library Cataloguing in Publication Data

McMullen, Alex
    Motor boating.
    1. Motorboats
    I. Title
    623.8'231

    ISBN 0–906754–38–0

Acknowledgements

I would like to thank Tom Willis, my successor as editor of *Motor Boat
& Yachting* magazine, and Tim Davison, of Fernhurst Books, for asking
me to write this book, and for their support and encouragement
throughout the project. I would also like to thank Tom and his staff for
their work in first publishing the book as a series in the magazine. In
particular, technical editor Tim Bartlett gave me much expert advice,
especially on the subjects of engines and maintenance.

Lester McCarthy, *Motor Boat & Yachting's* staff photographer,
provided nearly all the photographs, many of them taken specially for
the book. Most of the line illustrations were drawn by Margaret Nelson
in the magazine's art studio.

John Astbury of HM Coastguard advised me on some of the finer
points of radio procedure, which is described in chapter 8. Two trailer
manufacturers, Indespension and Lew-Ways, helped me with
information on boat trailing, the subject of chapter 12.
                                                    Alex McMullen

Photographic credits

Lester McCarthy of *Motor Boat & Yachting* took most of the
photographs in this book, and the picture that appears on the cover.
The boat handling photographs (chapter 3) were taken by the author.
Cloud photographs (chapter 7) by courtesy of the Meteorological
Office. Other photos by Jonathan Eastland (motor cruiser in heavy
seas, chapter 9) and Janet Harber (cargo boat in narrow channel,
chapter 4).

Design by John Woodward
Composition by Central Southern Typesetters, Hove
Artwork by PanTek, Maidstone
Printed by Ebenezer Baylis & Son, Worcester

Contents

1 Choosing a boat

Before you choose a motor boat you should ask yourself three questions:

1. Where am I going to do my boating—in coastal waters, inland waterways, or both? If in coastal waters will I be in an area of deep-water harbours or one where most places dry out at low tide?

2. What do I want to do in my boat—dayboating, weekending, cruising, fishing? If a mixture of some or all of these, what's the priority?

3. Do I want a boat that's fast—to get me from A to B as quickly as possible or just for the pleasure of high-speed boating—or would I rather sacrifice speed in the interests of economy, or to give myself a greater range and perhaps a more seaworthy boat for serious offshore cruising?

Other factors have to be considered, too, of course, like the all-important cost, but your answers to the three questions above will help you make the critical choices about the type of boat you want: its hull shape; its engine (or engines); and its interior and exterior layout. You won't, at least if you are buying new, have much choice about the construction of your boat. Nearly all modern motor boats are made of glass reinforced plastic.

You may have to make compromises, if for instance you are going to be boating both inland and on the sea, and your choice may be limited by what's available. But knowing what would have been your ideal boat will help you to know the limitations of what you end up buying. And there's no harm in having ideals.

HULL SHAPES

The shape of hulls is infinitely variable, but there are three basic types: displacement; planing; and semi-displacement, sometimes called semi-planing.

Displacement hulls are so-called because, even when under way, they follow Archimedes' basic rule of physics that a floating object displaces its own weight in water. When it moves through the water a displacement hull sets up a wave pattern that limits its speed in knots to approximately the square root of the waterline length in feet multiplied by 1.4. Thus a boat with a waterline length of 20ft (6.1m)—overall length about 23ft (7m)—will have a maximum displacement speed of about 6¼ knots, while a boat of 30ft (9.1m) l.w.l.—overall length, say, 35ft (10.7m)—will manage about 7½ knots.

As it travels through the water, a displacement boat effectively rests on two waves that move apart as speed increases. Try to push the speed above $1.4 \times \sqrt{\text{l.w.l.}}$ and the stern wave drops behind the boat, which is left climbing the bow wave at an attitude that is both uncomfortable and very expensive in fuel.

Planing and semi-planing boats overcome this natural speed barrier by a combination of greatly increased power and a hull form with which they can lift themselves partially clear of the water.

Displacement motor boats are either 'round-bilge', with underwater sections like a wine glass that curve down to a long, shallow keel; or 'hard-chine' with a shallow-vee bottom and a long keel. They are easily and economically driven, up to their maximum hull speed, and tend to be better than planing boats in rough seas, when speed has to be reduced.

Unfortunately, very few boatbuilders turn out displacement boats these days, but there are plenty on the secondhand market.

In theory a flat bottom would be the most efficient hull shape for planing. But a flat-bottomed boat, and its crew, would take an unacceptable beating as it slapped into waves, and its handling would be wayward to say the least. Most planing boats have a chine hull, with a sharp angle (the chine) between the topsides and bottom, and a vee-shape bottom that is a compromise between a good planing surface and a shock absorber. Racing boats and some high-performance cruisers have deep-vee hulls in which the deadrise (the angle between the horizontal and the hull) is a constant 20° or more, but most planing boats have a variable deadrise: steep forward and shallowing towards the stern, where wave-induced motion is least, to an angle of only 10–15°. This hull form is called warped bottom—a phrase you will rarely see in sales literature!

Designed for high speed, vee-hulled boats are not so happy at displacement speeds, when they lack the directional stability of a boat with a keel, and so

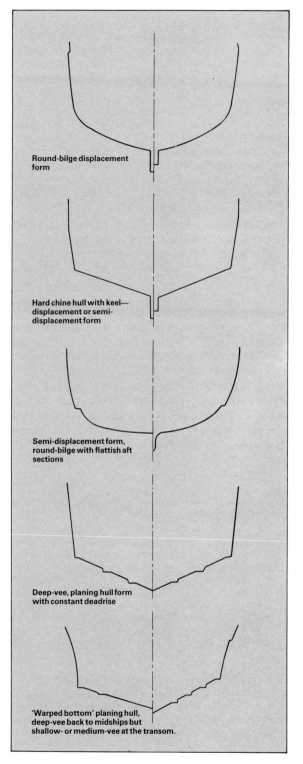

Round-bilge displacement form

Hard chine hull with keel—displacement or semi-displacement form

Semi-displacement form, round-bilge with flattish aft sections

Deep-vee, planing hull form with constant deadrise

'Warped bottom' planing hull, deep-vee back to midships but shallow- or medium-vee at the transom.

◄ Hull sections—stern on the left, midships on the right.

are harder to steer. They are not so good, therefore, on inland waterways with speed restrictions, or at sea when the going gets so rough that you have to come off the plane. The best planing boats can stay on the plane in all but the most extreme conditions, but many start to slam uncomfortably in anything over force four or five in exposed waters. With caution and careful planning you are less likely to get caught out by bad weather in a fast boat, but it will happen sooner or later, probably sooner if you undertake any serious cruising.

Semi-displacement or semi-planing boats, as their alternative names suggest, combine characteristics of both displacement and planing boats. Usually they are round bilge with a keel but with flat or flattish sections aft. They are not as efficient as true planing boats when planing, or as displacement boats at displacement speeds, but they lack the vices of the specialist craft and some of the best designs have an excellent reputation for good seakeeping.

Many motor boats fall into a grey area between planing and semi-displacement. Several, for example, have a planing hull form and a very shallow keel. This improves directional stability but decreases the boat's top speed slightly. And there are other designs that don't follow the norms outlined: small planing boats that have one of the various forms of trihedral hull and get lift from the tunnels between the outer sponsons and the central hull section; and traditional canal boats with flat or nearly flat bottoms that depend for directional stability on their great waterline length (relative to their beam) rather than on a long keel.

ENGINES

In deciding on the ideal engine installation you have to make three choices: one engine or two; diesel or petrol; and inboard, outboard or outdrive (inboard engine driving an outboard leg). On some types and sizes of boat the choice is not so complicated. Only a few boats under 25ft (7.6m) long have room for two inboard or outdrive engines, while 20ft (6.1m) is the lower limit for two outboards. At the other end of the scale, not many fast cruising boats over 35ft (10.7m) are fitted with anything but twin diesel inboards. But in between you can take your pick of boats with all possible combinations, though single or twin diesel outboards are a rarity. Many builders offer the choice of diesel or petrol engines in their boats, sometimes single or twin engines and, more rarely, the option of inboard or outdrive, or outdrive or outboard.

A twin-engine installation is undoubtedly a useful safety feature as long as it doesn't lead to complacency —if you don't look after your engines they may both fail you. It has the further advantage of increasing a boat's manoeuvrability. Don't, however, confuse manoeuvrability with positive low-speed handling, essential for inland cruising and best achieved by a large rudder behind a single propeller.

Single-engine installations do have a number of advantages which should be weighed against the get-you-home benefit of a second engine. One engine takes up less room and so is more accessible. On a boat with a keel a single propeller is given a measure of protection which is rarely the case with

▶ Outboard engine.

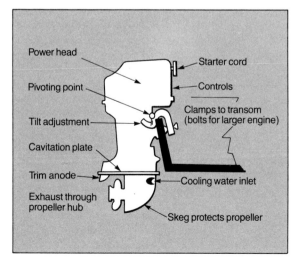

▶ Outdrive or sterndrive.

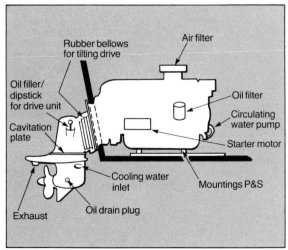

9

two props. For extended inland cruising a single, protected prop on the centreline is far preferable to two props that are unprotected and that little bit nearer the shallower water towards the bank. Bear in mind too that, on an inboard-powered boat, your propellers need to be protected if you are going to keep your boat on a drying mooring or are likely to want to visit drying harbours and anchorages.

On most boats up to about 30ft (9m) there is a way of having two-engine reliability with only one main engine: keep an outboard engine in a cockpit locker and fit a bracket for it on the stern.

In deciding between diesel and petrol you have to weigh up the merits of each. Petrol engines are lighter, cheaper to buy and quieter. Diesel engines are more reliable, cheaper to run and safer. Some of that needs qualifying: the difference in weight and noise levels between diesels and petrol engines is lower than it was a few years ago. And to say that diesels are safer doesn't imply that petrol engines are inherently dangerous, just that petrol is considerably more inflammable than diesel and fire precautions, such as the installation of a remote, preferably automatic engine-room extinguishing system, need to be taken. It is the electrics on a petrol engine that most commonly give rise to trouble on boats; electrical devices don't like water, especially salt water.

The differences in capital and running costs are very significant. Diesels cost between one and a half and three times more than petrol engines to buy and about half as much to run, but you have to cover several thousand miles in a diesel boat before you can offset the fuel savings against the additional

capital outlay. Most boats do less than 500 miles a year. Another consideration is that, in many areas, petrol is a lot less readily available than diesel.

Inboard engines, driving a propeller shaft, are the most efficient of the commonly used means of propulsion. But outboards and outdrives have a number of advantages on boats up to about 25ft (7.6m) and 35ft (10.7m) respectively. Both are easier and cheaper to install and they save space (the outboard more so in each case). You can also raise the propeller—very useful for clearing it of obstructions and when you want to dry out. Outboards up to about 40hp are also portable. On the debit side, because you steer outdrive and outboard boats by turning the propeller and directing its thrust, steerage at low speed is poor, so they are not very suitable for canals and rivers. You can fit rudder attachments, but they are never as good as a proper, decent-sized rudder.

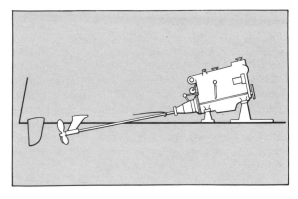

One half of twin inboard installation with P-bracket holding the propeller shaft.

Single inboard engine (amidships mounting).

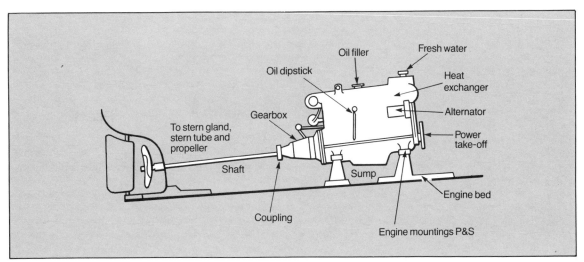

⬥ **Shetland Family Four.** A 17ft 7in (5.36m) fast, trailable cruiser for sheltered waters or offshore in set-fair weather. Single outboard up to a maximum of 90hp; 50hp would still give 20 knots. Simple two-berth cabin.

⬥ **Sealine 215.** A 21ft 4in (6.55m) fast cruiser, trailable behind large cars. Choice of single petrol or diesel outdrives up to 225hp, giving 30 knots plus. Accommodation for four, with two more in the canopied cockpit.

⬥ **Hardy Fishing 24.** A 24ft (7.3m) semi-displacement fisherman. Cockpit big enough for eight anglers and small cabin to sleep two. Single or twin inboards, outdrives or outboards up to 120hp, giving speeds of 20 knots plus.

⬥ **Sunseeker 27 Monterey.** A 27ft (8.2m) Mediterranean-style cruiser with large cockpit and accommodation under the foredeck for two. Deep-vee planing hull. Wide choice of diesel and petrol outdrives. Top speed with single 200hp petrol engine 33 knots, or 36 knots with twin 150hp diesels.

◗ **Elysian 27.** A 27ft (8.3m) displacement river cruiser (but capable of estuary and fine-weather coastal hops). Choice of single inboard diesels of 35-50hp, all giving displacement hull speed of about 7.5 knots. Accommodation for four.

◗ **Princess 30DS.** A 30ft (9.1m) fast cruiser from towards the bottom end of the extensive Princess range. Hull deep-vee forward, medium-vee aft. Twin petrol or diesel inboards or outdrives up to 420hp total. Top speeds from 20 knots to 30 knots plus. Six berths. Enclosed wheelhouse/saloon.

◗ **Broom 9/70.** A 32ft (9.7m) semi-displacement cruiser suitable for river and coastal work. Diesel inboards from one at 130hp, giving 10 knots, to two at 260hp giving 18 knots. Inside and outside helm positions. Four berths in two separate cabins plus settee/berths in saloon.

◗ **Pedro 33.** A 33ft (10m) steel displacement cruiser from Holland, land of the steel boat. Single or twin diesel inboards from 60hp. Top speed restricted to maximum hull speed of 8 knots. Dual helm positions in wheelhouse/saloon and aft deck. Accommodation for six.

◆ **Birchwood TS33. A 34ft (10.4m) medium-vee-with-keel planing cruiser. Twin petrol or diesel inboards from 200 to 400hp total, giving up to 25 knots top speed. Inside and outside helm positions; accommodation for six.**

◆ **Weymouth 34. A 34ft (10.4m) semi-displacement, round-bilge cruiser noted for good seakeeping in rough seas. Twin diesel inboards up to a total of 450hp, giving top speeds of up to 25 knots. Accommodation for six or seven.**

DECK AND INTERIOR LAYOUT

If most of your boating is going to take the form of fair-weather day trips you want a boat with a reasonable amount of open space in which to enjoy the sunshine. If fishing is your game you want a spacious uncluttered cockpit. But if you plan to undertake much cruising then a comfortable interior with enough sleeping and living accommodation for you and your crew is the priority requirement. Beware of the claims of some builders and dealers; a six-berth boat may have six berths, but is there room for six people to stow their gear, eat, sit and generally live together for several days and still remain friends?

Many motor cruisers over 30ft (9m) have the luxury of dual helm positions, one out in the open on a flying bridge or raised aft deck, the other in the warmth and comfort (and poorer viewpoint) of an enclosed wheelhouse. In boats of under 30ft it's usually one or the other, or a third option of some kind of open-backed wheelhouse. Again, the choice depends on the kind of boating you are going to do, as well as the depth of your pocket.

CONSTRUCTION

Nearly all modern motor boats are built of glassfibre, or to give the material its more precise name, glass reinforced plastic. Steel is still deservedly popular for canal boats, being a much better material to withstand abrasion from lock sides and banks. And the Dutch produce some good seagoing displacement cruisers in steel. The number of yards turning out

♦ **Fairline 36 Aft Cabin.** A 36ft 6in (11.2m) deep/medium-vee fast cruiser in the 21-50ft Fairline range. Choice of twin 200 or 300hp diesel inboards, giving top speeds of 23 and 27 knots respectively. Inside and flying bridge helm positions. Accommodation for six.

♦ **Grand Banks 42.** A 42ft (12.8m) 'trawler yacht'. Basically displacement form, but flat underwater sections enable semi-displacement performance with twin diesel inboards of up to 375hp each. Top speed of 22 knots. Sleeps six.

wooden cruisers can be counted on the fingers of one hand. The still relatively new epoxy-saturated wood construction method, producing the attractive looks of a wooden boat with the low-maintenance benefits of glassfibre, has so far been largely restricted to small open craft such as reproduction steam boats. You can, of course, still buy wooden boats secondhand.

WHERE TO LOOK

The pages of boating magazines are as good a place as any to start, whether you are looking for a new boat or a secondhand one. All the leading magazines carry advertisements placed by builders and dealers in both new and used boats. The reviews of new designs will also give you a feel for the market. If you want to buy secondhand put your name down with brokers in your area, and with any others who seem to sell the type of boat you're looking for.

Boat shows are an invaluable shop window for new boats. A few offer the opportunity of a trial run, at least in some of the boats on show.

You don't have to buy a boat to get afloat; you can charter. There's no shortage of boats for hire on the inland waterways, but the number of seagoing charter motor boats is limited; many are skippered, and thus more expensive, while 'bareboat' charter operators require some evidence of previous experience. There are other ways of getting afloat and gaining experience at the helm before you set off into the blue and this will be one of the subjects covered in the next chapter.

2 Ready to go

You've found a boat you like. Now you need to establish whether she is soundly built and, if secondhand, whether she has been well maintained.

Buying new, you can gain some assurance if the boat is from a known, reputable builder, but there are more positive indications of good construction. Some boats are built to one of the various certifications by Lloyd's Register or one of the other marine classification societies, such as Bureau Veritas or Det Norske Veritas. Some builders offer the option of a Lloyd's Hull Construction Certificate, at extra cost, and even if you don't take up the option you know that their construction drawings and their premises have been approved by Lloyd's surveyors.

Before buying a secondhand boat it is well worth paying for a professional survey. Find a surveyor, either from the classified section of a boating magazine or by contacting a professional association (see the list of addresses).

Always arrange a trial run before buying new or secondhand. If you know someone who is reasonably knowledgeable about boats take him or her along, not just for their knowledge but for a second, perhaps more dispassionate opinion. Find out whether a magazine has published a report on the boat you are thinking of buying and see if you can get hold of a copy.

BOAT BUYING

Some builders and dealers still expect their customers to spend several thousand pounds with no more precise an agreement than a simple invoice. You should insist on the use of one of the standard forms of agreement for the purchase of a new boat, obtainable from the British Marine Industries Federation or the Royal Yachting Association; this will detail the terms of payment, including stage payments if you are buying a boat before or during construction.

When buying secondhand you need to establish that the vendor has full title to the boat—that there are no outstanding mortgage payments, for example. If the boat has been registered (under the Merchant

Shipping Act, 1894, not the simplified Small Ships Register) it is easy enough to check. If buying privately use the RYA's form for a secondhand sale agreement and ensure that it states that no other party has any claim on the boat. Most brokers have their own forms of agreement, standardised under the code of practice to which they are bound.

If you need to borrow money for your boat you can, for a small craft, raise a loan from a bank or finance company. For more expensive boats you will probably have to apply for a marine mortgage from a specialist marine finance house, payable over a period of up to fifteen years.

REGISTRATION

In the UK you don't have to register a boat, but you must do so if you cruise overseas. There are two forms of registration: what is called 'full registration', under the Merchant Shipping Act of 1894, through the Registrar of Shipping (or local registrars in the official ports of registry, usually to be found in the Customs & Excise offices); and a greatly simplified, and cheaper version under the Small Ships Register (SSR), which is run by the Royal Yachting Association. SSR registration is accepted by most European countries,

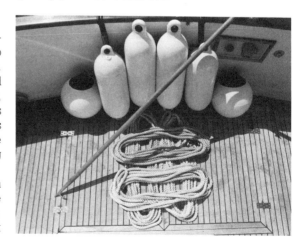

◆ **Warps, fenders and boathook.**

though it is no more than a declaration of ownership. Full registration, which gives evidence of title, is advisable for prolonged stays in a foreign country and is usually insisted upon by finance companies before they give marine mortgages.

If you use your boat on the inland waterways you will have to licence her with the appropriate river or canal authority.

INSURANCE

You should insure your boat for her full value and with third party cover. Premiums vary from about 1% to 3% of a boat's value.

It is best to deal with a recognised marine insurance broker. Most policies are based on the standard Lloyd's marine policy, with what are called the Institute Yacht Clauses. The most important of these concern cruising range, duration of use (eg April to October) and speed—the speedboat clause imposes certain conditions, and a higher premium, on boats designed to do more than 17 knots. Take great care in both taking out your policy and, when you have it, in reading the small print.

EQUIPPING YOUR BOAT

Builders and dealers sometimes claim that their boats are 'ready for sea'. They never are. One or two of the critical safety items will almost certainly be insufficient in number or size—or won't exist at all. And there is always plenty of less important, but nonetheless essential gear to be bought.

Tender If you are going anywhere where you have to anchor or pick up a mooring buoy you will need a tender to get ashore, either a solid dinghy or an inflatable. It can be powered by oars or a small outboard engine. Solid dinghies tend to be easier to row, but inflatables, except when light-loaded in strong winds, are more stable. The favoured method of stowing a tender is over the stern in davits, from which it can be easily launched and retrieved.

Warps, fenders and boathook You need at least four mooring warps, two of at least 30ft (9m) and two at least 50ft (15m)—more and longer on boats over 30ft. The best material is polyester, though polypropylene, lighter and not quite so strong, is acceptable on small boats. It's a good idea to carry one or two longer, nylon warps as well, as extra anchor line, or for towing (or being towed). At least six fenders are required of appropriate size for your topsides, including a couple of fat, spherical ones, particularly if you have flared topsides forward. Buy a stout boathook (or two), long enough to reach a mooring buoy or low quayside from deck level.

Anchor The two most popular types are the Danforth and the Plough. The anchor and anchor line must be heavy enough for your boat (see the table overleaf). Nylon rope is an acceptable, weight-saving alternative to chain, but have at least 15ft (4.5m) of chain at the anchor end to provide the weight to help the anchor stay buried. Carry at least 100ft (30m) of chain or warp, more if you are undertaking serious cruising. Carry another anchor as a spare and as a possible second anchor in strong winds or to minimise movement in a very restricted anchorage.

◄ A tender on stern davits.

◄ A Danforth anchor (left) and plough anchor (right).

Minimum anchor and anchor line sizes for Danforth and plough anchors			
Boat length ft (m)	Anchor wt lb (kg)	Chain dia in (mm)	Warp dia mm
15 (4.5)	10 (4.5)	¼ (6)	10
20 (6)	15 (7)	¼ (6)	10
25 (7.5)	20 (9)	5/16 (8)	12
30 (9)	25 (11)	5/16 (8)	12
35 (10.5)	35 (16)	5/16 (8)	12
40 (12)	40 (18)	3/8 (10)	16
50 (15)	55 (25)	7/16 (11)	18

NB: These figures are for craft of average displacement, anchoring only in sheltered anchorages, with good holding.
Heavy displacement boats or boats undertaking extended cruising should carry heavier anchors and larger-gauge anchor lines.

Radar reflector One of these will improve your chances of showing up on another vessel's radar. The octahedral type is the cheapest, but it must be hoisted in the correct 'catch-rain' position. More effective (and more expensive) types are available.

Horn Every boat must have a horn, either a fitted electrical one or a portable, compressed-air type.

Bilge pumps Standard equipment on new boats often includes an electric, submersible pump, usually fitted with an automatic float switch, but every boat should also have a manual pump. Fit one if one

◆ Electric (left) and manual (right) bilge pumps.

➥ An electric horn.

➥ A brace of radar reflectors: the traditional octahedral type, solidly mounted in the correct 'catch-rain' position (left) and a modern encapsulated model.

isn't already fitted. It should be somewhere in the cockpit in a position where it is easy to use. If your boat has separate bilge compartments there should be a submersible pump in each and you should fit a manual pump with a movable suction hose or one with separate suction hoses and a change-over valve.

Navigation lights Port (red) and starboard (green) sidelights, masthead light and sternlight (both white) should be standard equipment on any boat that

might be underway at night. On boats under 40ft (12m) the masthead light and the sternlight can be combined in an all-round white light, and boats under 23ft (7m) don't have to have sidelights (but should if they can). The exact requirements for navigation lights will be covered in Chapter 4.

Steering compass Make sure it is easy to read from the helm position, yet not surrounded by magnetic influences. There should be a built-in light for night work. Check the compass for deviation and if necessary have it adjusted.

Hand bearing compass You will need one of these to help you plot your position when coastal navigating and for other purposes which will be mentioned later in the book. Choose a compass you find easy to use.

▲ Navigation lights are obligatory for cruising by night.

◄ The steering compass must be mounted with care, away from magnetic influences and clearly visible from the helm.

Speed and distance log Another vital aid to navigation. Some logs show speed on an analogue dial, others in digital form. Check the accuracy, at different speeds, on a measured mile, remembering to do two-way runs to eliminate the effects of any tidal streams.

Echo sounder When navigating inshore you need to know the depth of water you are in. Echo sounders are a vital—and surprisingly inexpensive—navigation aid. There are various types, giving analogue or digital readouts, or both. Another type, favoured by fishermen and divers, gives a visual display of the ups and downs of the seabed, and any shoals of fish you are passing over.

◄ An electronic digital log (left), digital/analogue depth sounder (right) and rudder angle indicator (below).

◗ A hand-bearing compass is an essential aid to navigation and to collision avoidance.

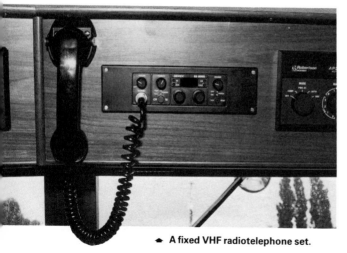

↤ A fixed VHF radiotelephone set.

↤ A Decca-type electronic navigator.

VHF radiotelephone An aid to safety and a useful tool for talking to other boats and to harbours and marinas. If you don't have the space for a fixed VHF you can buy a portable set. You need a licence and must take an exam to get an operator's certificate. You should also have a good radio receiver on board, to listen to shipping forecasts.

Rudder indicator Boat handling is a whole lot easier if you can tell whether your helm is to port, to starboard or midships. It's surprising how many boats don't have a rudder indicator to give that information.

Chart table, instruments and books You need a parallel rule, or one of the many patent plotting devices; dividers for measuring off distances; pencils; a rubber; a nautical almanac; and a logbook. Plus, of course, charts and pilot books.

↦ Charts, plotting instruments and almanacs.

Decca-type navigator A piece of electronic wizardry that, if you are in a Decca area (like northern Europe), will give your position, in latitude and longitude, and will give you a course to steer to a given 'waypoint', with a constant flow of information about the distance to travel, estimated time of arrival, and distance and direction of course. A very useful navigational aid, but dangerous if you come to rely on it and neglect the basic navigation skills—electronic aids like this can and do go wrong.

Radar The advent of cheaper, smaller and easier to use radars has made them a practical proposition for many boat owners, in boats of about 25ft (7.6m) upwards. They can be a great aid to safety in bad visibility and a useful navigation aid, but they require considerable skill to operate correctly. Used incorrectly radar can be more of a hazard than a help.

↦ Radar is becoming increasingly common in small boats.

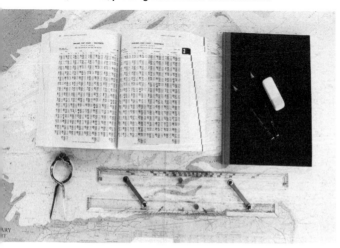

An autopilot is a blessing on a long haul.

A lifebuoy held securely in its mounting bracket.

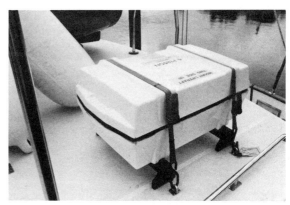

A canister-type liferaft mounted on deck.

Lifejackets must be the right size to be effective.

Autopilot For long passages an autopilot can take a lot of the strain, enabling the helmsman to concentrate on keeping a good look-out.

Binoculars Not just for bird watching; binoculars are a useful navigation aid, for identifying buoys and other navigation marks. 7 × 50 is the favoured size, but 8 × 30 is fine. More powerful models such as 10 × 50 are difficult, from a boat, to hold steady on a small distant object.

Lifebuoys Install a couple of lifebuoys on holders from which they can be instantly removed for throwing to anyone who falls overboard. They should *not* be attached by a line to the boat. They can be fitted with an automatic light and a whistle, attached so as not to hamper throwing.

Liferaft Any boat that does more than purely local, inshore summer boating should have a liferaft, big enough to take everyone on board. Liferafts come in solid canisters which can be mounted on deck held down by quick-release straps, or in a valise which can be kept in an easily-accessible deck or cockpit locker.

Lifejackets Seagoing boats should have enough lifejackets for however many people are likely to be on board; enough adult-size ones for the adults and the right size children's jackets for each child. Lifejackets should conform to BS 3595 and be of the permanent buoyancy type for children. Lifejackets or buoyancy aids, which give less support than lifejackets but are generally much less bulky and more comfortable, should be carried by boats cruising on the larger inland waterways.

◆ Carry a full set of flares—and find out how to use them!

◆ Fire extinguishers of the right type are essential equipment.

◆ Mount a fire blanket within easy reach of the cooker.

Distress flares For coastal cruising carry at least two red parachute flares, two red handheld flares and two orange smoke flares. For local inshore boating you could manage without the parachute flares, which are designed to be seen from considerable distances. Offshore you should have at least another couple of red parachute and red hand flares. White flares, not for distress but for attracting attention, can also be useful.

Fire extinguishers and fire blanket Boats up to about 30ft (9m) should have at least two easily accessible 3lb (1.4kg) fire extinguishers, preferably of the

dry powder type. Larger boats should have more, including at least one 5lb (2.3kg) extinguisher. Engine-rooms are best served by their own extinguishers, of the BCF type. Ideally they should be remotely controlled but in high-speed petrol installations they should be automatic. Cooking fat and other galley fires are often most effectively extinguished with a fire blanket. Fit one on a bulkhead within easy reach of the cook.

First aid kit Specialist first aid kits are available, or you can make up your own, ensuring that it caters sufficiently for the most common boating ailments, like burns, sunburn, stomach upsets, and seasickness, and for any medical problems to which you and your crew are prone. Keep everything neatly packed in a waterproof container, make sure everyone on board knows where it is, and regularly check the contents, replenishing as necessary.

Tool kit Carry adequate tools to cope with minor repairs to your engine(s) and equipment. Include: spanners, screwdrivers, hammer, pliers, hacksaw (and blades), hand drills (and bits), Allen keys and Mole grips. Some engine manufacturers offer sets of tools to suit their engines, and these may form a good basis for a tool kit. A good folding knife with a marlin spike is another essential item.

Spares For engines: drive belts, hoses and hose clips, water pump impeller, gasket set. Plus, for diesels, injector and injector pipe; for petrol engines, spark

◆ Always keep a well-stocked first aid kit on board.

▲ **The set of tools provided by an engine manufacturer will often form a basis of a good toolkit.**

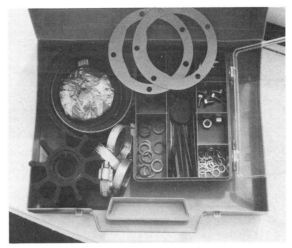

▲ **You can never carry too many spares and odd items.**

▲ **Equip yourself as well as your boat!**

plugs, set of points and coil; for outboards, propeller and (as appropriate) shear pins and split pins. Electrical spares, bulbs and fuses; cable connectors. And don't forget such items as fuel filters, lubricating oil, distilled water, and if appropriate, sterntube grease; or maintenance items like light oil, WD40, general purpose grease, adhesives, plastic tape and insulating tape.

Waterproof clothing Not so much equipping your boat as equipping yourself. Essential gear includes a waterproof jacket and trousers, as well as shoes with good non-slip soles, and plenty of warm clothing.

GENERAL

Boats that are only going to be used on inland waterways don't need the same range of navigation aids as seagoing boats, but most of the equipment is relevant to all boats. Even canal narrowboats should have an anchor if they are ever going to venture on to river navigations—think of it as a brake in the event of engine failure.

On a seagoing boat the most important item of equipment is the steering compass. This should be swung (checked) and a card drawn up showing any deviation (caused by the boat's local magnetic field) on different courses. It is possible to carry out a rough check yourself, using transits (charted landmarks in line) or comparing the boat's compass with a hand bearing compass, held well away from any possible magnetic influences. The compass's correctors should be adjusted if the deviation is more

than two or three degrees. Before undertaking any serious cruising you should have your compass swung and adjusted by a professional.

TRAINING SCHEMES

The Royal Yachting Association has devised a range of courses for skippers and crews of motor boats, and a number of motor cruiser schools and clubs give practical and theoretical training up to the standards of the various certificates. Details of the courses, together with syllabus booklets and lists of schools and clubs, are available from the RYA. The RYA, while we're on the subject, supports the interests of all boating people, whatever size and type their boats, from boardsailors to offshore racers. It is well worth supporting in return, by becoming a member.

Many clubs also organise boat handling competitions and cruises in company. Crewing in a friend's or fellow club member's boat is an excellent way of gaining experience.

Several boat dealers offer a day or more of tuition to their customers, in the boats they have just bought. This can be a useful addition to some other, more comprehensive, form of training and will help you familiarise yourself with the handling of your boat.

FINDING A MOORING

Moorings are as varied in their type as they are in their cost. You will need a bank loan to pay the mooring fee at some marinas.

At the other extreme, in some areas (well away from the crowd, and almost certainly in a harbour that dries out at low tide) you can moor to a buoy for the cost of laying and maintaining it.

USEFUL ADDRESSES

British Marine Industries Federation, Boating Industry House, Vale Road, Oatlands Park, Weybridge, Surrey KT13 9NS. Tel: 0932 854511
Royal Yachting Association, RYA House, Romsey Road, Eastleigh, Hants SO5 4YA. Tel: 0703 629962.
Yacht Brokers, Designers and Surveyors Association, Wheel House, 5 Station Road, Liphook, Hampshire GU30 7DW. Tel: 0428 722322.

If you know where you want to keep your boat make local enquiries. Otherwise consult one of the published guides to coastal and inland moorings. You can of course avoid the problem of finding a mooring if you have a boat that can be trailed and somewhere to keep it.

FLAG ETIQUETTE

It is usual practice, for cruising boats anyway, to fly at least two flags: an ensign and a club burgee. In most countries the ensign is simply the national flag, but in the UK it is either the Red or Blue Ensign, never the Union Jack. Most boats fly the Red Ensign but members of certain clubs can obtain a warrant to fly a Blue Ensign or a Red or Blue Ensign defaced with a club symbol. Ensigns are usually flown at the stern.

Club burgees, which are usually triangular or (for club commodores, rear-commodores or vice-commodores) swallow-tailed, are flown by sailing yachts at the masthead or by motor boats as high as possible, perhaps on the steaming light support if there's no signal mast.

If you cruise to a foreign country you should fly a small version of the country's ensign when in its waters, preferably at the starboard crosstrees if you have a mast.

PRE-START CHECKS

Before you cast off, not just on your maiden voyage, but on every outing thereafter, you should make a number of checks on the boat, engine(s) and equipment. Draw up a checklist to suit your own boat, but make sure you include the following:
- Turn on the gas detector (if fitted).
- Check bilges and pump out if necessary.
- Check fuel level(s).
- Check radio and navigation aids.
- Check engine and gearbox oil levels.
- Check freshwater cooling level(s).
- Turn the sterntube greaser (if fitted), refilling if necessary.
- Check the steering.
- Close portholes, low-level windows and deck hatches.
- After starting engine(s): check cooling water flow, oil pressure and battery charging.

---

3 Boat handling

The art of handling your boat smoothly and precisely can only be achieved with practice. Practice makes perfect, but an understanding of the theory about how a boat moves through the water will speed your progress to perfection.

Driving a motor boat is not like driving a car, and it's not just the absence of brakes. You turn the helm (wheel) the same way as in a car: clockwise to turn to starboard, anti-clockwise to turn to port—and vice versa going astern—but a boat does not just turn to port or to starboard, she pivots about a point. Going ahead, that point is well forward of amidships, so the stern swings to starboard on a port-hand turn more than the bow swings to port.

Going astern, the pivot point moves aft so the bow describes the greater arc. The situation is complicated by other factors: rudders (on inboard-engine boats) are much less effective when the propeller stream is not flowing past them; and most boats, if it's blowing hard, will tend to turn stern to wind when moving astern.

Then there's paddlewheel effect: the sideways kick of a propeller as you engage gear and start to move ahead or astern. Most single-engined boats have right-handed propellers (turning clockwise viewed from aft) which will kick the stern to starboard as you go ahead, to port going astern. Twin-engined boats should have contra-rotating, preferably 'outward' turning props, ie, right-handed starboard and left-handed port. Paddlewheel effect is thus eliminated when both engines are in forward or astern gear, and when turning a boat by putting one engine in forward gear and one in astern the paddlewheel effect of both operates in the same direction—the direction of the turn.

You must also take into account the action of wind and tide (or current on a river). How they affect a boat will depend on the shape and size of her superstructure and underwater hull respectively.

As far as the lack of proper brakes is concerned, try not to think of going hard astern as an exact equivalent. Consider the welfare of your gearbox; slip into neutral to slow down, or apply only minimum astern power, unless there is an emergency.

➤ **Manoeuvring your boat into position in a marina can be a real test of your boat handling skill.**

◀ Turning a single-inboard boat in a restricted channel. With a right-handed propeller it is best to turn to starboard to benefit from paddlewheel effect in both forward and astern gear. Apply helm before power for maximum turning effect and least forward movement. In the middle photo astern gear is engaged while the boat is still swinging.

MANOEUVRING

Every boat has its own handling characteristics, and there are marked differences between boats with inboard engines and either outboards or outdrives, and between single and twin engine boats.

Single inboard

A boat with one inboard engine and one rudder is the easiest of all types to handle so long as she is moving forward, but the most difficult in any kind of man- oeuvre that involves stopping and starting, because she depends on forward movement for steerage. She has virtually no steerage going astern, at least not in the first few, vital yards of any manoeuvre.

When turning and going forward, for maximum effect put the helm over in the desired direction *before* engaging gear; if possible, before going astern get the bow swinging in the desired direction by giving a burst ahead with the helm over. Don't turn the helm the other way until the boat starts to move astern.

Because paddlewheel effect is more marked when you engage astern gear it is generally best, in a boat with a right-handed propeller, to complete a three- point turn in a clockwise direction, ie, turning to star- board first, then going astern. Slip into neutral and then go hard astern while the boat is still swinging; a combination of that swing and paddlewheel effect will help the boat to continue turning in the right direction as you gather sternway.

Single outboard or outdrive

Because you steer outboard- and outdrive-powered boats by turning the propeller rather than a rudder, their handling characteristics are very different from inboard boats. For a start they can be steered quite effectively astern by putting the wheel (or outboard

◆ In an outboard or outdrive boat you can make very tight turns by putting the helm hard over and then applying power (left). Since the propeller turns as you put the helm over, you can also steer very effectively in astern gear, but you have no steering at all in neutral. As before, engage astern while the boat is still swinging (right).

tiller) hard over before applying power. Paddle-wheel effect is not so noticeable as in an inboard boat, at least when the propeller is at an angle.

When cruising at low speed, steerage is less positive than on inboard boats, which is not so good for canal and river work. When you slip into neutral, to take off speed when approaching a lock for example, you lose steerage altogether. A rudder attachment on the lower unit can give you limited out-of-gear steerage, but should not be used at high speeds.

Twin inboards

In twin-engine boats each engine, because it is off-set, has a turning force. This is cancelled out by the other when both are working in the same direction, but can be used to good effect when manoeuvring. Because they often have small and, at low speeds, not very effective rudders, it is best when turning in a restricted space to put the helm amidships and steer using the engine controls only.

By going ahead on one engine and astern on the other you can spin the boat round in her own length. Use low revs, ideally just engaging gears on tickover, not applying heavy bursts of power.

Twin outboards or outdrives

When manoeuvring a boat with two outboard or sterndrive engines you can treat it like a single outboard/outdrive boat or one with two inboards, or you can combine the tight turning characteristics of both by turning the wheel and playing the engine controls. This can be very effective but it requires considerable concentration and experience.

◆ With twin inboard engines you can virtually turn the boat on the spot using only the engine controls. With the port engine ahead, starboard engine astern and wheel amidships the boat executes a graceful pirouette. You need very little power; a tickover is sufficient, which is why there is no wake showing in these photographs.

COMING ALONGSIDE

Before approaching an alongside berth, gauge the strength and direction of the tide (or current) and the wind. You should always approach heading into the tide, or if the tide is very weak or non-existent, into the wind. That way the operation is slower and more controlled, and as you head in towards the berth the tide, or wind, will help push you in. The skill to develop is knowing when to turn to leave the boat parallel to the berth and close enough for your crew to step off with your mooring lines.

Against a strong tide or wind you should approach at a shallower angle than the normally recommended 30°, to avoid being spun round. Strong crosswinds should also be taken into account. A wind blowing on to your berth can be used to push you in—take it extra slowly and turn parallel to the berth in good time—while in a wind blowing off the berth you must make sure you get close in before turning, to avoid being blown off.

In a restricted space, such as a marina with finger pontoons, give yourself room to manoeuvre by keeping well up-tide, or up-wind, of other boats and obstructions. You may, in a marina, have to enter a berth with the tide or wind, or both, behind you. More than ever, in such circumstances, you need to take things very slowly and to know just how your boat reacts to the helm and engine controls.

Always put fenders out and prepare bow and stern lines in good time. Lines should be led from the cleats to which they are secured, through the fairleads, under any guardrails and back over the top, then coiled neatly ready for throwing.

Single inboard

Paddlewheel effect must be taken into account; with a right-handed propeller it can be used to help you get alongside when berthing port-side to, but has to be counteracted when berthing starboard-side to. Going port-side to, head in at the normal 30° to the berth. When you engage astern gear to slow down, paddlewheel effect will help turn the boat parallel to the berth. Starboard-side to, approach at a shallower angle. You will need to oversteer to port, because when you go astern the paddlewheel effect will try to push your stern out.

♦ Coming alongside in a single-inboard boat with a right-handed prop. As in any type of boat always approach into the wind or tide, whichever is the strongest. Port side to, in astern gear to slow down, paddlewheel effect will help kick your stern in. Starboard side to, the paddlewheel effect works against you, so approach at a shallower angle.

Single and twin outboards and outdrives

Simply apply the general rules for coming alongside, and the techniques described under 'manoeuvring'. With practice, the ability to turn an outboard or outdrive boat—in particular to push the stern sideways —without much forward or astern movement can be used to very good effect.

↪ **Coming alongside in an outboard (or outdrive) boat.** Approaching at about 30 degrees to the quay you can go quite close at very low speed. Then, when in neutral, turn the helm to port (if port side to), and apply a burst of astern power to swing your stern in.

Twin inboards

Make the final approach on engine controls only, with helm amidships, slowing down and turning by slipping into neutral on the inside (berth-side) engine and going astern on the outside engine, working the controls as necessary to make fine adjustments to your speed and angle.

↪ **Coming alongside in a twin inboard boat.** Using engine controls only, and on a bare tickover, approach at about 30 degrees and go astern on the outer engine to bring the stern in. You can use the same method with twin outboards or outdrives, but using the wheel as well may help.

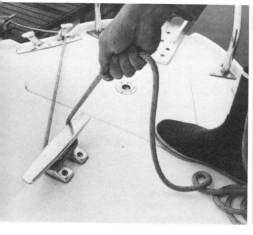

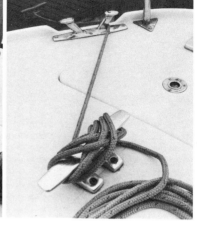

● Before throwing a line ashore, coil up enough to reach the shore, splitting it between your throwing hand (as many coils as you can comfortably hold and throw) and your other hand (held on an open palm so they will run out freely).

● When securing a rope to a cleat take it to the 'far' end first, then take a turn round the bottom before laying on figure-of-eight turns, finishing off with another turn round the bottom (as here) or with a half hitch.

MOORING UP

Secure the bow and stern lines first, making sure that the bow line runs ahead of the boat and the stern line runs aft, so they keep the boat from moving in either direction. To hold the boat more securely in place add springs as well; a fore spring running from the bow aft and an aft spring running from the stern forward. In tidal waters, remember to adjust your lines as the tide rises and falls (unless you are moored to a floating pontoon); the longer all the lines are, the less they will need adjusting.

Ensure that fenders are well secured, at the right height and distribution to protect your topsides. If you are moored outside another boat don't just tie on to her; take additional bow and stern lines ashore.

● A line is best attached to a bollard using a bowline (see the knot diagrams overleaf). If putting a line on an occupied bollard take the end of yours through any other lines before looping it over; this allows others to cast off without removing your mooring line first.

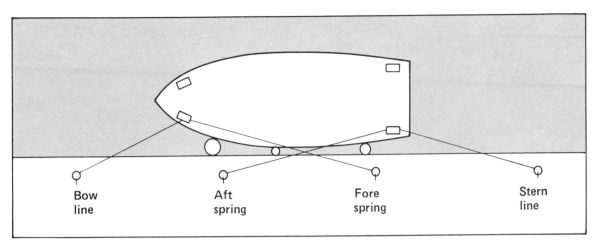

| Bow line | Aft spring | Fore spring | Stern line |

● Fore and aft springs stop the bow and stern from swinging outwards in the current, and help to hold the boat snugly against the quay. You can run them from the bow and stern cleats, as here, or from a single midships cleat.

● A well-moored and fendered boat with long bow and stern lines and bow and stern springs. The fenders attached to the bases of the guardrail stanchions have been adjusted to the right height for the pontoon.

→ To get into a tight marina berth, get a bow spring on to the pontoon first. Take a turn around a cleat or bollard and use the line as a brake if necessary.

→ The four most commonly used knots: a round turn and two half hitches, for securing a line to a post; a clove hitch, for the same purpose but less secure; a bowline, the best way of making a loop to drop over a cleat; a double sheet bend, for joining the ends of two ropes together.

UNBERTHING

When leaving an alongside berth (unberthing is the correct, if not very attractive term) you can make the tide or wind work for you by going out bow first if you are head to it, or stern first if it's running (or blowing) from astern.

Think about the order in which you cast off your lines. Springs are usually cast off first, leaving until last whichever of the bow or stern lines is holding the boat against the tide or wind. This final line should be set up as a slip rope (through a ring, or round a bollard or cleat, and back to the boat) so that it can be released from on board.

You can use your lines to help extricate yourself from a tricky berth. For example, if berthed in a tight space with other boats close ahead and astern, you can drive your bow off by motoring astern against a fore spring (rove as a slip rope), or drive your stern off by going ahead against an aft spring.

Leave your fenders in place until you are comletely clear of the berth; indeed, before you unberth check that you are well fendered in the appropriate places, at the bow if going out stern first, at the stern if going out bow first. Once you are well clear of the berth don't forget to take all your fenders in and coil and stow all your lines.

→ Springing out of a tight berth. This twin-engined boat uses an aft spring to go out bow first; as it motors slowly astern on starboard engine the spring stops it running back into the boat astern while the bow swings out. The line is run back to the boat so it can be retrieved from on board.

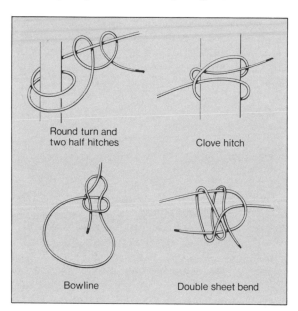

Round turn and
two half hitches   Clove hitch

Bowline   Double sheet bend

↞ It is often best to leave a berth stern first; because of their shape most boats will swing that way when alongside. However, if you are heading into a strong current or wind, push the bow out and the current (or wind) will do the rest.

↞ You can use your lines to get out of a tight marina berth, expecially in a single-inboard boat. Here the stern line, doubled up and controlled from the boat, is used to motor against and help swing the stern round to port.

PICKING UP A BUOY

The crew member who's up on the foredeck to pick up a mooring buoy should help guide the helmsman to the buoy by pointing at it, perhaps with the boathook. This is especially important as you get close and the helmsman loses sight of the buoy under the bow.

If possible approach against the tide or wind. Judge when to stop the boat so that the foredeck crew can easily reach the buoy with the boathook or, in a small boat, with his or her hands. In a single-engined boat allow for paddlewheel effect, which will turn the bow to starboard as you engage astern gear to slow down.

ANCHORING

Check against the chart and pilot book that an anchorage is safe—that the holding is good and the bottom free of hazards—and calculate how much the tide is going to rise and/or fall while you are at anchor (charts, pilot books and tides will be covered in Chapter 5). Using your echo sounder, pick a spot where you are neither going to touch bottom at low tide nor have too much water under you at high tide. Check also that the anchorage is sheltered.

Prepare the anchor in good time, ensuring that the chain (or warp) is free to run out. It's a good idea to lay out some chain on the foredeck. By snaking it down in metre lengths—charts and tide tables are in metres so always think metric when calculating depths—you can see how much has run out, even if you don't have it marked.

Once again, approach into the tide or wind, going ahead of where you want to end up, letting go the anchor and enough chain for it to hit the bottom, then rapidly letting out more as you drop back—with some gentle help from the engine if necessary. You should have let out three times the depth of water in chain, or five times the depth in warp. Let out more as the tide rises, or make sure you have enough out in the first place for the depth at high water.

Check that your anchor is not dragging by noting any clear transit (objects in line) ashore and checking that it remains as a transit. Alternatively, take a compass bearing on something ashore and check that the bearing doesn't change. As far as possible, take transits and bearings at right angles to the likely direction of drag.

→ **Accurate steering and a light touch on the engine controls pay dividends when entering or leaving a lock.**

MEDITERRANEAN MOORING

In the Mediterranean, and in one or two places in northern Europe, the conventional system of mooring is stern to quay. You anchor or pick up either a buoy or a line running out from the shore, then drop back to secure two stern lines ashore. You then adjust the lines to leave a gap between stern and quay that can be bridged by a passarelle (boarding plank). In the Med there's no tide to worry about, but stern-to mooring can still be a severe test of your boat-handling skills.

LOCKS

One can only give rough guidelines for boat handling in locks—they vary so much in size and type. Taking a boat into and out of a lock calls for precise steering and working of the engine controls. Line the boat up for the final approach and slow right down, but not so much that you lose steerage. Watch out for cross currents from sluices and weirs. In an inboard-powered boat take speed off by going briefly into neutral. If you have to go astern to slow down, paddlewheel effect will quickly knock you off course.

Incidentally, in twin-inboard engine boats it is usually easier to hold your course by steering with the wheel, not with the engine controls. If the two engines, even at tick-over, push you along too fast put just one engine into gear—you can counter its turning movement with the wheel. Outboard and outdrive boats are much more difficult to handle because, unless you have a rudder attachment, you lose steerage in neutral. But with practice you get a feel for it and can cope with locks quite adequately.

Always be prepared to moor up on either side— have fenders out both sides and be ready to switch your lines across. Once alongside, get your lines ashore as quickly as possible. When entering a full lock it is often best to get your stern line on first; there may be a slight current through the lock which will try to carry you on towards the far gates.

Don't forget to take up the slack in your lines as you rise in a filling lock, and, more importantly, don't forget to let them out in an emptying lock. Have them as slip ropes if they are long enough.

Going down, keep well away from the top gates to avoid being suspended on the upper level cill as the lock empties, and ensure that no part of the boat is overhanging the lock side or, if you have gone to the far end of the lock, any part of the bottom gates. Going up, check that no part of the boat is in danger of being caught under any overhang.

4 Rule of the road

People talk about the freedom of the sea, and it's the lack of constraints and controls that is one of the main attractions of going to sea in a boat.

Nevertheless you have to obey the 'rule of the road', otherwise known as the collision regulations or more accurately, and dauntingly, the International Regulations for Preventing Collisions at Sea. Harbour authorities impose their own regulations, and then there are the unwritten rules of courtesy and common sense. Inland waterways have their rule of the road too; a mixture of common practice, common sense and navigation authority regulations.

You don't have to learn the collision regulations by heart—they run to several thousand words—but you should know the following rules about collision avoidance, the lights and shapes shown by vessels of different types and different activities, and sound signals. Here is a precis of those rules, with explanatory notes

➡ **If you have to give way take early and substantial action. This way the helmsman of the other vessel knows what you are doing.**

where necessary. The full wording—and the complete rules—can be found in the almanacs and various reference works.

COLLISION AVOIDANCE

● Always keep a good look-out (Rule 5).
● Always proceed at a safe speed, taking into account visibility, traffic density, sea conditions, proximity of navigational hazards and the depth of water (Rule 6).
● Use all available means to determine if the risk of collision with another vessel exists (Rule 7). The best way to do this is to take compass bearings of the other vessel in question. Unless they change significantly there is a risk of collision.
● Any action taken to avoid collision—an alteration of course or reduction of speed—should be positive (Rule 8). In other words, make it clear to the other vessel that you are taking avoiding action. The

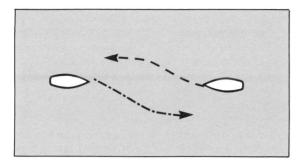

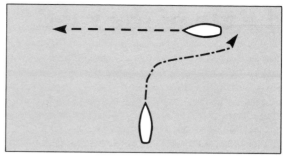

↞ **If two vessels are in danger of colliding head on, they should turn to starboard and pass port side to port side.**

↞ **If two vessels are on a converging course the one that has the other on its starboard side should give way.**

question of who should be taking avoiding action is covered by Rules 12 to 18.

● In narrow channels keep to starboard and keep clear of a vessel which can safely navigate only within a narrow channel or fairway (Rule 9).

● In traffic separation schemes (shipping lanes) proceed in the correct lane; enter if possible at the end of the lane, otherwise at as shallow an angle to the lane as practicable; crossing shipping lanes should be avoided if possible but if you have to cross them do so at right angles to the direction of traffic (Rule 10). Traffic separation schemes are clearly shown in charts. It is best when coastal cruising to use inshore traffic zones, outside the shipping lanes.

● Rule 12 concerns sailing vessels only, but it's as well to know it; basically it states that a boat on port tack—with the wind on her port side—gives way to boats on starboard tack, and when two boats are on the same tack the one to windward gives way.

● You must give way to any vessel you are over-taking, ie approaching from more than $22\frac{1}{2}°$ aft of its beam (Rule 13).

● When two power-driven vessels are in danger of colliding head on both shall alter course to starboard, to pass each other to port (Rule 14).

● When two power-driven vessels are crossing and in danger of colliding, the one which has the other on her starboard side shall give way, if possible by turning to starboard to pass astern (Rule 15).

↞ **In a narrow channel you must keep to starboard, and stay clear of any vessel that is restricted to the deep water owing to its greater draught.**

● If you have to give way to another vessel take early and substantial action (Rule 16).

● If you have right of way you should hold your course, unless it's clear that the other vessel is not taking action to avoid a collision (Rule 17). If you want to avoid a close encounter with, say, a large ship, in a situation where you will have the right of way, take avoiding action well in advance, before the ship is obliged to do so.

● Power-driven vessels should give way to sailing vessels and both should give way to vessels not under command, restricted in their ability to manoeuvre, or fishing (Rule 18). Sailing boats only have right of way over motor boats if they are under sail only. 'Not under command' means unable to manoeuvre. Vessels that are 'restricted in their ability to manoeuvre' include those laying buoys or cables, dredging, surveying and, in many cases, towing or being towed.

LIGHTS AND SHAPES

● Lights (as specified in Rules 21 to 30) must be shown between sunset and sunrise, and in daytime bad visibility; the specified shapes should be shown by day (Rule 20).

● Definitions: a 'masthead light' is a white light showing ahead and to 22½° aft of the beam; 'sidelights' are red (to port) and green (to starboard) lights showing from dead ahead to 22½° aft of the beam on each side; a 'sternlight' is a white light showing astern over an arc of 135°, ie the sector not covered by the masthead light (Rule 21).

● On vessels up to 40ft (12m) long the masthead light and sternlight must be visible for at least two miles, sidelights for at least one mile; on vessels between 40 and 65ft (12–20m) long the masthead light must be visible for three miles, the sidelights and sternlight for two miles (Rule 22).

● When under way, power-driven vessels under 165ft (50m) long should have one masthead light, sidelights and a sternlight; vessels under 65ft (20m) can carry sidelights combined in one lantern. On motor boats under 40ft (12m) the masthead light and sternlight can be combined in one, all-round light. Motor boats under 23ft (7m) long can exhibit just an all-round white light but should show sidelights (separate or combined) as well if practicable (Rule 23). Combined sidelight lanterns should be carried on the centreline (at least 3ft 3ins (1m) below the masthead or all-round light); separate sidelights are preferable.

● When under way, sailing vessels (under sail only) need to show sidelights and a sternlight; in boats under 65ft (20m) long these can be combined in one lantern at the masthead; in addition (but not with a combined sidelights/sternlight lantern) they can shown red over green all-round lights at or near the masthead (Rule 25).

● Vessels at anchor should show one all-round light, or by day a black ball. Vessels under 23ft (7m) long, if anchored away from a narrow channel, fairway or anchorage, are exempt. Vessels over 40ft (12m) when aground should show two red all-round lights in a vertical line or, by day, three black balls in a vertical line (Rule 30). The black ball rule is widely ignored by small craft, nor do many yachts over 40ft

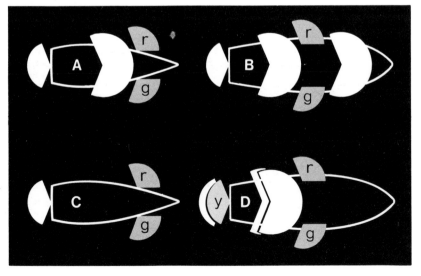

◆ The lights shown by vessels under way: (A) A power-driven vessel under 50m (165ft) long. If under 12m (40ft) the white masthead light and sternlight can be combined. (B) A power-driven vessel over 50m long. The forward masthead light is lower than the aft one. (C) a vessel under sail only. In boats under 20m (65ft) all the lights can be combined in one masthead lantern. (D) A vessel towing, with two masthead lights and a yellow towing light above the sternlight. When the total length of the two is more than 200m three masthead lights are shown. The vessel being towed shows just sidelights and a sternlight.

(12m) carry two all-round red lights and three black balls to hoist in the rigging. But there are occasions where such signals could be very useful; a black ball, for example, would be useful if you were forced to anchor, say through engine breakdown, in a busy fairway.

● Rules 24 and 26 to 29 specify the lights and shapes to be shown by towing—and towed—vessels, fishing vessels, vessels not under command or restricted in their ability to manoeuvre, vessels constrained by their draught and pilot vessels.

SOUND AND LIGHT SIGNALS

● Definitions: a 'short blast' lasts about one second, a 'long blast' from four to six seconds (Rule 32).

● Rule 34 specifies the sound signals that power-driven vessels should make when manoeuvring and giving warnings to other vessels. The manoeuvring signals should be made 'when vessels are in sight of one another'. This should not be taken literally by small craft, or the sound of boats' horns would be just about constant in many places—but occasionally it is necessary to indicate to another boat what you are doing, and you should know what the signals mean when you hear them sounded by the ships and other large craft that do use them as a matter of course. The short-blast signals may be supplemented by equivalent light signals.

● Rule 35 specifies the sound signals that should be made in bad visibility. These should not be ignored by anyone, particularly in thick fog in areas where there are likely to be other ships or boats about.

◗ Lights and shapes indicating specific activities.

◗ Sound signals for bad visibility and when manoeuvring. Small craft rarely need to make manoeuvring signals.

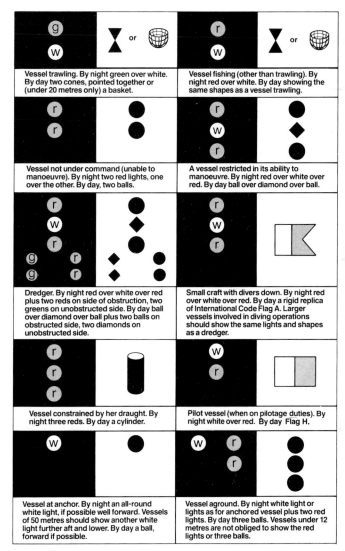

Vessel trawling. By night green over white. By day two cones, pointed together or (under 20 metres only) a basket.

Vessel fishing (other than trawling). By night red over white. By day showing the same shapes as a vessel trawling.

Vessel not under command (unable to manoeuvre). By night two red lights, one over the other. By day, two balls.

A vessel restricted in its ability to manoeuvre. By night red over white over red. By day ball over diamond over ball.

Dredger. By night red over white over red plus two reds on side of obstruction, two greens on unobstructed side. By day ball over diamond over ball plus two balls on obstructed side, two diamonds on unobstructed side.

Small craft with divers down. By night red over white over red. By day a rigid replica of International Code Flag A. Larger vessels involved in diving operations should show the same lights and shapes as a dredger.

Vessel constrained by her draught. By night three reds. By day a cylinder.

Pilot vessel (when on pilotage duties). By night white over red. By day Flag H.

Vessel at anchor. By night an all-round white light, if possible well forward. Vessels of 50 metres should show another white light further aft and lower. By day a ball, forward if possible.

Vessel aground. By night white light or lights as for anchored vessel plus two red lights. By day three balls. Vessels under 12 metres are not obliged to show the red lights or three balls.

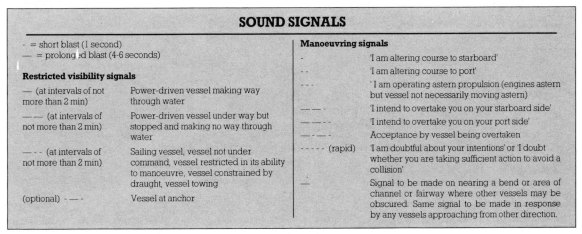

SOUND SIGNALS

		Manoeuvring signals	
- = short blast (1 second)		-	'I am altering course to starboard'
— = prolonged blast (4-6 seconds)		- -	'I am altering course to port'
Restricted visibility signals		- - -	'I am operating astern propulsion (engines astern but vessel not necessarily moving astern)'
— (at intervals of not more than 2 min)	Power-driven vessel making way through water	— — -	'I intend to overtake you on your starboard side'
— — (at intervals of not more than 2 min)	Power-driven vessel under way but stopped and making no way through water	— — - -	'I intend to overtake you on your port side'
		— - — -	Acceptance by vessel being overtaken
— - - (at intervals of not more than 2 min)	Sailing vessel, vessel not under command, vessel restricted in its ability to manoeuvre, vessel constrained by draught, vessel towing	- - - - - (rapid)	'I am doubtful about your intentions' or 'I doubt whether you are taking sufficient action to avoid a collision'
(optional) - — -	Vessel at anchor	—	Signal to be made on nearing a bend or area of channel or fairway where other vessels may be obscured. Same signal to be made in response by any vessels approaching from other direction.

● If you want to attract the attention of another vessel use light or sound signals that cannot be mistaken for any signal authorised for another purpose, or for any navigation aid (Rule 36). A white hand flare is the best method of attracting attention to yourself, in the event, say, of another vessel bearing down on you when you are unable to get out of the way.

● Rule 37, and Annex IV, cover the internationally accepted distress signals. Some, like the burning of tar or oil in a barrel, are not to be recommended on small craft. The most commonly used distress signals are: the word 'Mayday' broadcast by radio-telephone; a rocket parachute flare or a hand flare showing a red light; an orange smoke flare; SOS in morse code (· · · – – – · · ·) sent by any form of light or sound signal, or (unlikely in small craft) by radio-telegraphy; a continuous sounding of the foghorn; the slow and repeated raising and lowering of outstretched arms; signals transmitted by an emergency position-indicating beacon. You should only use distress signals when in serious and immediate danger and requiring urgent help. The subject of distress and emergency will be covered in a later chapter.

HARBOUR REGULATIONS

Most harbours, and many estuaries, are governed by regulations imposing speed limits and restrictions on anchoring and mooring. Some have signals governing entry and departure; there is an international system of port traffic signals, but many harbours have their own. Check your almanac and pilot book for details and look out for noticeboards detailing any limits and restrictions.

RULE OF THE ROAD (INLAND)

On rivers and canals there are a number of conventions about passing, overtaking and rights of way that are internationally recognised. Some are based on the collision regulations. Often they are incorporated into a set of navigation authority rules, which will also lay down the law about other subjects, such as speed limits and where you can and cannot moor. The principal rules are:

● Keep to the right when passing other boats going in the opposite direction; ie pass port to port.

● On bends commercial craft may need to keep to the deep water on the outside, so be prepared when negotiating a left-hand bend to break the keep-to-

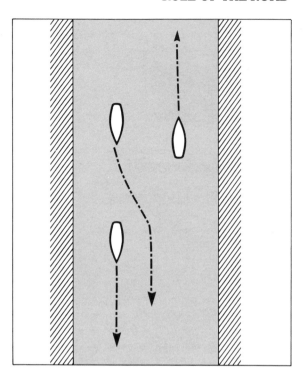

◆ On inland waterways you keep to starboard and overtake on the port side of the boat ahead. As in all narrow channels, you should always keep clear of any vessel constrained by her draught.

the-right rule and pass starboard to starboard. On the waterways of mainland Europe barges wanting other craft to pass them on the 'wrong' side put out a blue board to starboard.

● Overtake to port, leaving the overtaken boat to starboard. On canals and narrow rivers it is polite to indicate that you wish to overtake, and then await a come-on signal. Never overtake in narrow lock cuts or when approaching a bridge.

● Give way to all commercial craft, whether carrying cargoes or passengers. Don't attempt to overtake them when approaching a lock.

● Give way to sailing boats.

● When going up-stream on fast-flowing rivers keep well clear of craft coming downstream; they have less steerage way than you.

● Sound your horn as you approach a blind bend, and listen for responding blasts from any craft coming the other way.

● Slow down past moored boats and small open boats such as rowing skiffs.

● Watch your wash; if you are dragging a large wave behind you, especially if it is breaking against the bank, slow down.

● Do not moor near narrow bridges, immediately above or below locks (where boats waiting to go through may want to lie) or on bends.

● Find out what traffic signals there are (if any) at locks and tunnels, and observe them.

● Check the speed limit and do not exceed it.

UNWRITTEN RULES

Besides the obligations laid down in the collision regulations and local laws there are the conventions of courtesy and common sense which dictate a number of unofficial, but nonetheless, important rules of the road afloat.

● Slow down when you are passing moored or anchored boats.

● **Space is limited on inland waterways, and an inconsiderate helmsman can cause a lot of damage and make life very uncomfortable for everyone. Use your common sense, and keep your speed down.**

● Before mooring alongside another boat ask if you can do so.

● When anchoring make sure you end up well clear of other boats at anchor. In a motor boat you may not lie to your anchor in the same direction as a deep-keeled sailing yacht—a shallow-draughted motor boat will be more affected by the wind than a yacht, and less by the tide.

● Don't pass too close to other craft, especially small, open boats.

● Watch your wash and slow down if it is affecting other boats (whether under way or moored or anchored).

5 Buoyage, charts and tides

This chapter is by way of an introduction to the next, which will cover the techniques of coastal navigation. In looking at buoys and other navigation marks, at how the other features are drawn on charts, and at how to make tidal calculations we are really into the subject already. Such knowledge is essential to the art of getting from A to B at sea.

LIGHTHOUSES AND LIGHT VESSELS

Lighthouses mark prominent headlands and rocks, and as well as warning of danger their high profile makes them useful as landmarks on a coastal passage or as landfalls from seaward. Light vessels are found at some of the junctions and turning points of shipping lanes. Both have powerful lights with a distinctive revolving loom, which can often be seen when the light itself is beyond the horizon. The lights are usually white, but sometimes lighthouses have sectors of other colours to indicate an off-lying hazard or a deep-water channel.

IALA BUOYAGE

In Europe, navigation buoys—and often in shallow waters other marks such as posts—conform to the IALA 'A' Maritime Buoyage System, IALA being the International Association of Lighthouse Authorities. (In North and South America, and in parts of Asia, the IALA 'B' system prevails, with one important difference from IALA 'A'—see under Lateral marks, below.) There are four types of IALA mark:

Lateral marks are used to indicate either side of a channel: red buoys (usually can-shaped) or red posts to port, and green buoys (usually conical) or green posts to starboard when heading in the 'direction of the buoyage' which is always from seaward in channels approaching or inside harbours or estuaries. (Confusingly, the IALA 'B' system is the exact reverse, with red marks to starboard.) Otherwise the direction of buoyage is as shown on charts: a broad, outline arrow (around the UK it is generally from the south up the west and east coasts, and from west up the English

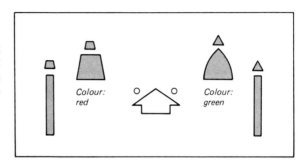

Lateral marks in the IALA 'A' buoyage system, marking a channel. Red cans to port, green cones to starboard, when heading in the direction of buoyage—usually from seaward heading inland. Where the direction is not obvious it is marked on the chart by an outline arrow, as illustrated. (Note that the system in American waters is the reverse.)

IALA cardinal marks, indicating some kind of hazard. North cardinal marks to the north of the hazard, east cardinal marks to the east, and so on. Note the distinguishing topmarks and colouring (yellow and black stripes), and the helpful light characteristics: quick or very quick flashing group 3 for east (3 o'clock); group 6 (plus long flash) for south (6 o'clock); group 9 for west (9 o'clock). North cardinals are continuous quick or very quick flashing. All lights are white.

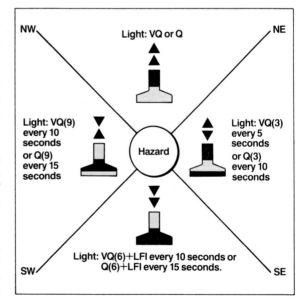

Channel). When lit, red marks have red lights and green marks green lights.

Cardinal marks indicate some kind of danger, like shallow water over rocks, a sandbank or a wreck; north cardinal marks to the north of the danger, east to the east, west to the west and south to the south. Rarely do you find all four round one danger. In European waters, cardinal marks have a distinctive pillar shape and the different marks can be distinguished by the arrangement of black and yellow bands and (more easily) by their topmarks; at night each has distinctive light characteristics, as shown in the illustration. The both-points-up and both-points-down topmarks of north and south cardinal buoys are easy enough to remember. There are various ways of remembering which is the west and which is the east topmark. The points-together topmark is 'W' for waisted; you can draw a small 'e' around the points-apart east cardinal topmark.

Isolated danger marks are just what the name suggests: single marks over an isolated danger of limited size. They can be passed on any side—but not too close.

Safe water marks are, again, what the name suggests, but more specifically they are usually mid-channel or landfall marks ('fairway' buoys are often safe water marks).

Special marks are not normally intended for general navigation (though they can be useful as waypoints on a passage or for fixing your position) but to show such things as military exercise areas, water-skiing areas, sewage outfalls (where the sewer itself is not a hazard), and tidal survey points. In some cases, where a normal navigational mark might be confusing, they do mark dangers and sometimes they are placed on the borders of traffic separation schemes.

LOCAL MARKS

Beacons and posts that pre-date the introduction of IALA marks (in the late 1970s and very early '80s) still serve as useful navigation marks in many estuaries and in many places on the coast.

Where relevant, and where practicable, they have often been painted and given topmarks and (if lit) light characteristics that conform with the IALA system. In some places you may still come across black conical buoys, the usual pre-IALA form of starboard-hand channel mark. Leading marks—pairs of posts or beacons that indicate the line of a narrow channel—are the other type of non-IALA local mark you will come across.

▶ **A typical south cardinal buoy, lit by solar power.**

▶ **Other IALA marks. Isolated danger marks can be passed on either side; if lit, the light is white, flashing group 2. Safe water marks can also be passed on either side; the light is white, isophase, occulting or one long flash every 10 seconds. Special marks are not intended as navigation aids; the light is always yellow, but otherwise variable.**

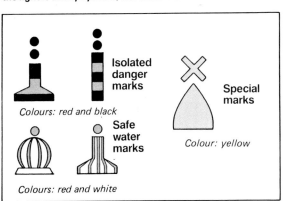

Isolated danger marks

Colours: red and black

Safe water marks

Colours: red and white

Special marks

Colour: yellow

CLASS OF LIGHT	INTERNATIONAL ABBREVIATION	OLD ABBREVIATION	ILLUSTRATION. (The period of each light shown thus ⊢────)
Fixed (steady light)	F	F	
Occulting (total duration of light more than dark)	Oc	Occ	
Group-occulting e.g.	Oc(2)	GP Occ(2)	
Isophase (light and dark equal)	Iso	Iso	
Flashing (total duration of light less than dark)	Fl	Fl	
Long flashing (flash 2s or more)	LFl	LFl	
Group flashing e.g.	Fl(3)	Gp Fl(3)	
Composite group-flashing e.g.	Fl(2+1)	Gp Fl(2+1)	
Quick flashing (50-79 flashes per minute)	Q	Qk Fl	
Group quick flashing e.g.	Q(3)	Qk Fl(3)	
Interrupted quick flashing	IQ	Int Qk Fl	
Very quick flashing (80-159 flashes per minute)	VQ	V Qk Fl	
Group very quick flashing e.g.	VQ(3)	V Qk Fl(3)	

◆ Common light characteristics, and how they are described on the charts. The old forms of abbreviation can still be found on many charts which, even though they have been corrected, may be old editions.

LIGHTS AND FOG SIGNALS

Lights vary in type and period, and to avoid confusion no two lights in a vicinity have the same characteristics. The principal types of light are shown above. The period of a light is the time from the beginning of one flash or group of flashes to the next, or, with occulting or isophase lights, one whole sequence of light and dark.

In bad visibility most lighthouses and light vessels emit one of the several kinds of fog signal. Some buoys are fitted with a bell, gong or whistle, usually activated by wave motion, so sounding in good visibility as well as bad.

CHOOSING CHARTS

Charts are basically maps of sea and coast, showing coastal features, navigational marks and charted depths (soundings). They have a built-in distance scale (one minute—⅟₆₀th of a degree—on the latitude scale up the side of the chart equals one nautical mile), a compass rose or roses—usually dual ones giving true and magnetic directions—and some limited tidal information.

Most of the world's vast area of sea has been charted by the Hydrographic Department of the British Admiralty. Admiralty charts are generally considered to be the best for the waters around the British Isles and, by British seamen and yachtsmen at least, for most other places. When purchased they are generally folded into two and rolled up. In the UK two independent companies produce their own,

folded charts, based on Admiralty surveys. They are sometimes more convenient than Admiralty charts, being of selected boating areas, on a fairly small scale but with large-scale inset charts of the principal harbours.

When buying charts for a cruise, or just to cover your local area, make sure you have small-scale (large-area) ones for the longest passages you are likely to make, and larger-scale ones for short coastal hops and for all the estuaries, harbours and anchorages you want—or may need—to visit. Also make sure they are up to date. Admiralty charts, if bought from an Admiralty chart agent, should be up to date when you buy them; independently-produced charts should be up to date when they leave the publishers, but may not be so if bought through a chandler. The Admiralty publish weekly *Notices to Mariners* and a quarterly *Notices to Mariners – Small Craft Edition* which give details of changes to charts.

CHART COLOURS AND SYMBOLS

The use of different colours helps distinguish land, areas that dry out at low tide, shallow water and deep water. On Admiralty charts the land is buff-coloured, drying areas are green, water of less than five metres charted depth (on some charts ten metres) is blue, the rest white, with a blue tint ribbon along the ten-metre depth contour (on some charts along the 20-metre contour).

Buoys and most other marks are shown on charts by stylised pictures of the appropriate shapes and topmarks so you can immediately see what type of

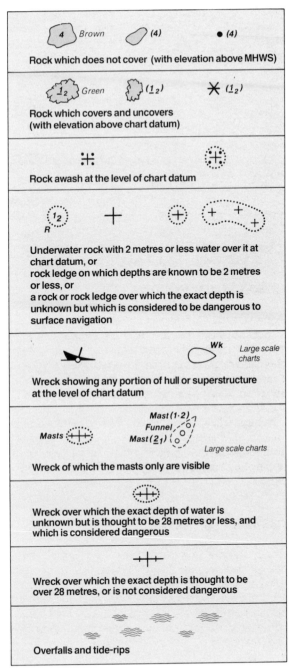

mark you are looking at (some beacons and posts are shown simply by a dot in a circle or, if lit, by an outline star and the abbreviation Bn). Marks with lights are shown with a magenta flare. The colour of the mark is shown (common colours by their first letter) and, if lit, the characteristics of the light, its colour (white if not stated) and if appropriate the period in seconds. For lighthouses and light vessels the elevation (height) and range (visibility) of the light are given, in metres (m) and nautical miles (M) respectively, and also the type and period of any fog signal. To use an Admiralty chart properly you really need to buy chart No. NP 5011, which is in fact a booklet, called *Symbols and Abbreviations used on Admiralty Charts*.

TIDAL DATA

When navigating in tidal waters you often need to calculate the depth of water, to know whether you can safely navigate across an area of shallows, or whether it is safe to enter a harbour that dries out or has a sand or mud bar across its entrance. Alternatively, you may want to work out the time at which the depth over shallows will be sufficient, or work out how far and quickly the depth is going to change where you want to anchor. And you may come across a bridge over tidal waters and have to calculate the clearance under it.

Tidal calculations can also be useful in helping you fix your position. When plotting a course or working out your position you will also need to know the direction and strength of tidal streams.

Some of the main symbols of danger as shown on Admiralty charts. The last wreck symbol is included for clarification; the absence of a dotted line indicates that there is no danger to small craft.
Top left: real life—the wreck of the ammunition ship *Montgomery*, off the River Medway.

Don't let all this put you off; with the information you get from a chart and appropriate tide tables none of these calculations are at all difficult.

A charted depth, or sounding, is the depth below chart datum. On most modern charts the chart datum is the sea level at lowest astronomical tide (LAT), the lowest low tide under normal weather conditions. In areas that dry out at LAT, charted depths take the form of drying heights (the height above chart datum), and are underlined. Charted depths on modern charts are in metres plus, in shallow water, tenths of metres. The depth of water at any given time is the height of the tide at that time plus the charted depth. Over drying areas the depth of water, if anything, is the height of tide *minus* the drying height.

Good tide tables give you the times and heights of tide at high water and low water every day (usually two of each) at 'standard ports', with difference at nearby 'secondary ports'. Remember that times are normally GMT, so you have to correct the time for seasonal variations such as British Summer Time.

Almanacs, some pilot books and most charts also give the heights of tide at mean (average) high water springs (MHWS), mean high water neaps (MHWN), mean low water neaps (MLWN) and mean low water springs (MLWS). From the tide tables you can quickly see when it's springs and when it's neaps by comparing the tide heights. The cycle from one

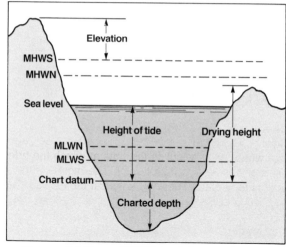

➤ Common tidal terms. MHWS stands for mean (average) high water springs, while MLWS stands for mean low water springs. MHWN refers to mean high water neaps, and so on. Note that the total depth of water is the height of tide *plus* the charted depth.

➤ With the tidal curve for your nearest standard port you can quickly work out the height of tide at any state of the tide, or the time at which the tide will rise or fall to a given height. Plot the low water and high water heights either side of the time in question and draw a straight line connecting them. Note the times of high water and hourly steps as appropriate. Then read off the height or time as indicated by the dotted line, using the solid line of the curve at springs and the pecked line at neaps (interpolate for periods between springs and neaps).

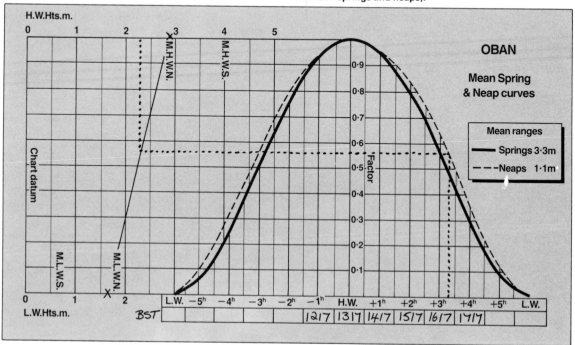

spring tide to the next is about fifteen days, springs occurring at full moon and new moon—when the gravitational pull of sun and moon combine—and neaps at the first and second quarter of the moon.

TIDAL HEIGHT CALCULATIONS

There are various ways to calculate the height of tide, and thus the depth, at times between high and low water, or to calculate the time at which the tide rises or falls to a certain height. The most accurate way is to use a tidal curve; a typical curve, and the method of using it, is shown in the illustration. Find the curve for the nearest standard port and plot the heights of tide for the low and high water either side of the desired time (they can be the heights at the standard port, or if nearer, one of its secondary ports). Draw a line between the two, then simply read across between the line and curve to find the desired height or time relative to high water.

Where the tidal pattern is regular you can calculate the *approximate* height of tide by simple arithmetic, using the 'Twelfths Rule'. On the flood the tide rises by $\frac{1}{12}$th during the first hour after low water and during the hour before high water, by $\frac{2}{12}$ths during the second hour after low water and the second before high, by $\frac{3}{12}$ths during the third hour after low water and third before high water. And vice versa on the ebb. It's a neat piece of symmetry which means that you simply have to work out the range of the tide (the difference between low and high water heights), divide it by the appropriate number of twelfths and add or subtract the result to or from the height at low or high water. For example, two hours after low water the tide will have risen by $\frac{1}{12} + \frac{2}{12} = \frac{3}{12}$ or $\frac{1}{4}$ of the range; if low water height is one metre and high water seven metres, the range is six metres, so the tide will have risen by $\frac{1}{4} \times 6 = 1.5$ metres; height of tide will be $1 + 1.5 = 2.5$ metres. And, just to recap, the depth of water will be the charted depth plus 2.5 metres. If you want accuracy, though, stick to tidal curves.

BRIDGE CLEARANCES

The 'elevation' (height) of bridges—and other overhead objects like power lines—is shown on charts as the height above mean high water springs. So, to calculate the clearance, if any, between the highest point of your boat and the underside of the bridge you need to know the height of tide at MHWS (from

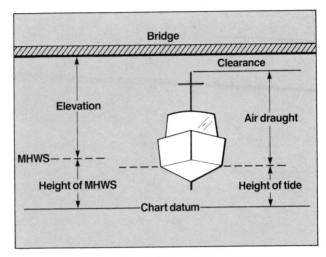

→ The factors involved in calculating whether or when you can pass under a bridge in tidal waters. See the simple formulae referred to in the text.

chart or almanac), the height of tide at the time you are planning to pass underneath (from tide tables and tidal curve) and your air draught (waterline to highest point). Use the following formula:

Clearance = (elevation of bridge + height of MHWS) − (height of tide + air draught).

If the answer is negative, don't attempt to pass under the bridge. The formula for calculating the maximum height of tide for safe passage under a tide-restricted bridge is even simpler:

Max height of tide = (elevation of bridge + height of MHWS) − air draught.

TIDAL STREAMS

There are two principal sources of information on the direction and speed of tidal streams. Most charts have a number of tidal stream diamonds, each with a letter in it; and in an inset box the tidal stream direction and speed at spring and neap tides, at each of those points, at hourly intervals related to the local standard port. The Admiralty's Tidal Stream Atlases (of which there are 15 covering British waters) have chartlets for every hour with the direction and speed in different places indicated by arrows and figures giving spring and neap rates in tenths of knots—hence 17,31 means a neap rate of 1.7 knots and a spring rate of 3.1 knots.

Clearly the tidal diamond figures are the most accurate as they give precise direction details, but they are only accurate for the area immediately around the diamonds.

For tides between neaps and springs it is usually good enough to interpolate—a third of the way from neaps to springs, a third of the way between the neap and spring rates. But you can use a table, called *Computation of Rates*, published in the Tidal Stream Atlases, if you want to be really accurate.

TIDES AND THE WEATHER

Strong winds and abnormal atmospheric pressure can upset your tidal predictions. Very strong winds funnelling into the Channel or down the North Sea, for example, can push heights up, or going the other way can make them lower than predicted. Very low pressure tends to cause the sea level to rise, whereas very high pressure causes it to drop. Sudden changes in wind direction can also affect tidal heights. Except in really extreme weather—unusual in the summer —such deviations from the norm usually amount to no more than half a metre. You should be aware of the problem, but you should in any case be building safety margins into your tidal calculations to allow for such phenomena.

6 Coastal navigation

At its simplest, coastal navigation involves nothing more than following a well-marked channel, or crossing a bay to a favourite anchorage. At its most advanced, it may involve a short sea crossing in bad visibility and strong tides, avoiding a dangerous wreck en route. At no level is coastal navigation difficult—it can even be enjoyable!

For an in-depth treatment of the subject, read *Inshore Navigation* by Tom Cunliffe (also published by Fernhurst Books), but this chapter should provide all the information you need for the first few passages.

In Chapter 5 we looked at some of the ingredients of navigation: a knowledge of buoys and other marks; charts, chart symbols and charted depths; and tidal calculations. In this chapter we will look at plotting courses on a chart, allowing for tidal streams, position fixing and pilotage, which is the art of navigating inshore, on short hops between navigation marks or clearly defined coastal features. But we will start with a couple of definitions that explain why one direction can be indicated by two, or even three different figures—remembering that a boat's course or the bearing of an object from a boat is given as the number of degrees clockwise from north.

VARIATION AND DEVIATION

Variation is the difference in angle between True North—geographical north, the 'top' of the Earth—and Magnetic North. It varies from place to place and, very slowly, with time. In northern Europe it ranges from 10° West on the west coast of Ireland to 8° East at Norway's North Cape; ie Magnetic North is between 10° to the west and 8° to the east of True North (in Great Britain it ranges from 9½°W along parts of the West Coast of Scotland, to just over 4°W in the extreme south east of England). To convert a True direction (°T) to magnetic (°M) you add the variation if it is to west or subtract it if it is to the east. 'Variation west, compass best; variation east, compass least' is a useful rhyme to remember.

Deviation is the difference in angle between Magnetic direction and the direction indicated by a compass which is affected by magnetic influences

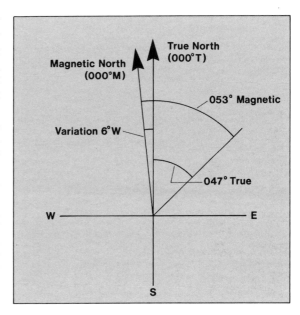

● Magnetic variation and the difference between True and Magnetic direction. With variation of 6°W a True course or bearing of 047° equals a Magnetic course or bearing of 047° + 6° = 053°. On the chart the local variation is usually shown as an inner circle on the compass rose, in smaller print.

● If a steering compass displays errors of more than 3° on any ship's heading it should be adjusted. Any remaining deviation should be recorded on a card like this, and kept somewhere near the compass.

DEVIATION CARD		
Magnetic Course	Deviation	Compass Course
000	1°W	001
045	–	045
090	1°E	089
135	2°E	133
180	3°E	177
225	1°E	224
270	1°W	271
315	2°W	317

on the boat. Deviation varies with the boat's heading and, as mentioned in the equipment checklist in Chapter 2, if a boat's steering compass deviates by more than two or three degrees on any course it should be adjusted. What deviation remains after adjusting should be recorded on a deviation card. Make sure that any loose magnetic objects, like beer cans, are always kept well away from the compass.

Note that, like variation, deviation is recorded as being west or east. If it is west, you add, if east, subtract, to convert from Magnetic to Compass (°C). So, as with variation, 'deviation west, compass best; deviation east, compass least'.

PLANNING A ROUTE

When planning any kind of coastal or estuarial passage you should always work out your courses in some detail. Read your chart carefully and plot a route that takes you well clear of any hazards, including shallow water. If possible stick to deep-water channels, but obviously in many very tidal areas—those with drying harbours, for example—that's impractical. Here it's essential to work out not only your route but when there will be sufficient depth to pass along it (making the necessary tidal calculations as explained in Chapter 5). Allow a large safety margin, especially if the tide is going to be falling.

As far as practicable, break up the passage into short legs between 'waypoints', which should prefer-ably be navigation marks, even if this means one or two slight detours. The shorter each leg, the less room there is for error.

Glean all the information and advice you can on the harbours or anchorages you plan to visit, from pilot books and from your nautical almanac. And at this stage make a note of what effect bad weather might have on your plans. Are there alternative routes more sheltered in certain winds? Which har-bours would make suitable refuges if the sea becomes too rough or if fog threatens?

Take into account also the effect of tidal streams. No need at this stage to work out course adjustments but, in a slow boat particularly, you want to calculate the best time to leave to avoid unfavourable currents, or, to put it more positively, to make use of favourable currents. And, however fast your boat, be aware of the effect of tide on sea conditions, especially if you are passing through any areas known to have tidal races or overfalls at certain states of the tide. Remember that wherever you are the sea will be rougher in 'wind against tide' conditions.

In well-marked channels, with closely-spaced buoys or posts, there is no need to plot courses on the chart, but you need to do so for the open water sections of any passage, even between waypoints half a mile or less apart. You don't know what the visibility will be like when you are out there, and you may need to know the course to steer and the exact distance. The best way to do that is, first of all, to draw a line on the chart.

PLOTTING A COURSE

Back in Chapter 2 the basic chart table instruments and books were listed. To recap, these are: parallel rules, or other plotting devices; dividers (preferably of the cross-over type that can be opened and closed with one hand); pencils; rubber; nautical almanac; the appropriate charts and pilot books; and a log-book. And, of course, you need a chart table, a fea-ture that's sadly lacking even in some quite large boats designed for cruising. If your boat doesn't have one, or a table of some sort suitable for chartwork, it would be a good idea to rig up a makeshift chart table, perhaps a collapsible one. It should be big enough to take an Admiralty chart folded in half.

Having decided on a course, say, between two buoys, draw a straight line between the two, or from just beside them on the side you need to pass.

Using parallel rules, step across to the nearest compass rose on the chart and read off and note the course. Parallel rules can be difficult to use on a

➤ **Working out a course, using parallel rules. Lay one edge along your route on the chart and step the rules across to the nearest compass rose. It will rarely be as simple as this; you will usually have to make two or three steps, each time holding one half down firmly while you move the other. When plotting a tidal set or bearing you do exactly the same, but starting at the compass rose.**

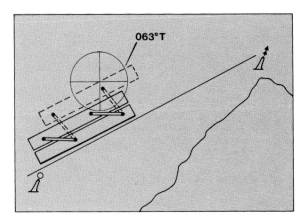

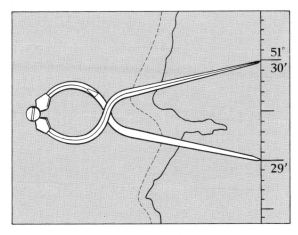

◆ Measuring distance on a chart is easy, using a pair of dividers and one of the latitude scales up the side of the chart. One minute (¹⁄₆₀th of a degree of latitude) equals one nautical mile. On large-scale charts each minute is divided into tenths, each equalling one tenth of a mile (a cable).

motor boat at speed or in rough weather, however, and most of the patent plotters have the advantage that they can be used to read off a course without you having to slide them across the chart.

Next measure and note the distance along your line, using dividers and the latitude scale up the side of the chart. This is a convenient distance scale, one minute (¹⁄₆₀th of a degree) of latitude equalling one nautical mile. Either put the dividers across the length of the line, if it's short enough to do so easily, and then go to the scale, or measure off a convenient distance on the scale and step along the course line.

You need to know the distance because once you are under way you will have to calculate your ETA (estimated time of arrival) at each waypoint. Checking that your waypoint comes up on schedule is one of the most basic elements of navigation. If your ETA arrives and there's no sign of the buoy you were heading for then you know, or must suspect, that your navigation is not what it should be—a much more likely answer than that the buoy has gone missing.

ALLOWING FOR TIDE

So far we have seen how to plot a course making no allowance for tidal stream, and that's all you need to do at the planning stage. But before deciding just what course to steer, and calculating your speed over the ground and your ETA at each waypoint, you must take the tide into account. From your chart or a tidal stream atlas work out the speed and direction of the stream, as explained in Chapter 5.

If the tide is running in the direction you are going, or if it's on the nose, then you won't have to worry about its effect on your course. Just note the speed and add it to or subtract it from your boat speed when calculating ETA. If, however, it is running across your path then you must allow for it. On a short leg, where your next waypoint is a clearly-identifiable navigation mark, you can do this by simply heading a few degrees up-tide of your plotted course and, by watching the mark (if possible against the coastline or some object behind it),

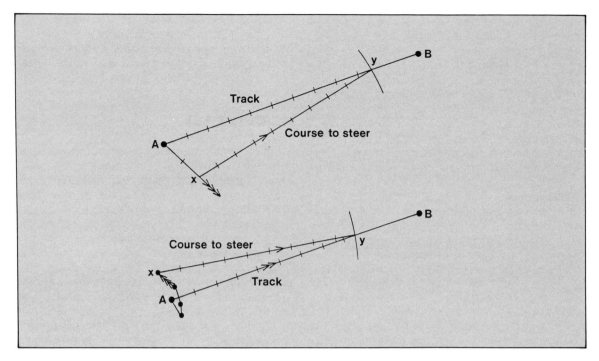

gauge your drift and make any necessary further adjustments to your course. On a fast boat—say over 18 knots—a weak tidal stream of half a knot or so is going to have very little effect, even if dead on the beam, and on any leg under three or four miles it can be ignored. But otherwise you need to calculate the effect of the tide. You can do this by drawing a tidal triangle, which is best explained by example. See the illustration above.

You can also be pushed off course by leeway, the effect of the wind on a boat's direction. Leeway can vary enormously, not just with the direction and force of the wind but from boat to boat. A boat with a deep keel and low superstructure—like most traditional displacement types—will be affected considerably less than a boat with a shallow keel (or no keel at all) and large upperworks—like most modern fast motor cruisers—which can suffer leeway of 5° or more in a fresh wind on the beam. Learn by experience how your boat is affected by leeway in different conditions, and make the necessary course adjustments.

On fast boats the plotting of courses, drawing of tidal triangles, or any kind of navigational calculation can be very difficult in a lumpy sea. The same goes for any kind of small boat in rough water. So the more detailed the planning the better. Once you know what time you are leaving on a passage, all the courses to steer and ETAs can be noted and you will

◆ **Working out a course to steer, allowing for tide, on a desired course ('track') from A to B. Plot the direction of the tidal stream ('set') as a line from A, then mark off the speed of the tide along the line in units of a convenient length. (If miles results in a ridiculously long or short line use, say, one tenth of a mile or five miles per knot.) From the resulting point (X) describe an arc across your track with your dividers opened up to the boat's speed through the water using the same units as for the tide. Draw a line from X to where the arc crosses the track (Y). XY represents the course to be steered and, measured in the same units, speed over the ground, from which you can calculate a revised ETA at B.**

In the upper example we have a boat travelling at 9 knots through the water, a tidal stream of 2 knots and, with a slightly favourable tidal stream, a speed over the ground of 9½ knots.

On long courses look up the tidal streams for different places and estimated times along the route. You can plot them together as shown in the lower sketch to indicate the overall effect of the stream.

Note the arrows, by convention single for course to steer, double for track and triple for tidal stream.

only have to rework your calculations if you get behind schedule.

DR AND EP

As important as the accurate working out of your course to steer is the ability to work out where you are at any time. If something goes wrong and you have to slow down or head for the nearest (safe) harbour you need to know from where to work out a new course. Or, if the worst happens and you have to put out a Mayday radio call, you need to be able to report your position as accurately as possible.

The simplest form of working out your position is by DR, which stands for dead reckoning. This means calculating from time and speed the distance travelled along a plotted course from the last waypoint. If you have an accurate allowance for tide and are travelling along your intended track the result is known as an EP or estimated position. But a better way to calculate your EP is to draw a tidal triangle, as shown in the diagram below.

If you have a distance-run log and if, as you should have done, you noted the reading at your last way-point, you can simply subtract that figure from the current reading. If not, knowing your speed and the time since you passed the waypoint, use the distance (nautical miles) = speed (knots) × time (hours) for-mula. On a long leg it is worth recording a DR or EP at regular intervals.

But speed and distance logs are often not very accurate and you may not have made the correct allowance for tide or leeway, or if you have had to allow for more than one speed and direction of tide you won't be running exactly along the course you have drawn on the chart. So take every opportunity to fix your position by other means.

POSITION FIXING

The best 'fix' is obtained by passing close to a navi-gation mark that you can positively identify—besides their shape, colour, topmarks and light characteristics most major marks display their names. But you can fix your position in other ways too. There are various radio and electronic aids, which we will look at briefly at the end of this chapter, but here we will concentrate on one of the basic skills of coastal navigation—fixing your position by visual sighting of seamarks and charted landmarks.

The most common form of visual fix is the taking of bearings of two, or preferably three, objects, and plotting the bearings on a chart. Ideally, for the greatest accuracy, the objects should be 120° apart if using three, 90° if using two. Three position lines should in theory cross at a point, which would be your fix, but in practice they always result in a triangle, called a cocked hat. If the triangle is reasonably small you can take the centre of it as your fix, or if you are close to some danger assume, for safety's sake, that you are in the nearest part to the danger.

Remember to take variation into account when plotting bearings. Deviation should not be a problem if you make sure that you hold your hand bearing compass well away from any magnetic objects, pref-erably somewhere out in the cockpit or, in calm water, up on deck. Practise using your hand bearing compass so that you are familiar with it.

The most reliable sort of position line is one derived from a transit: two objects—on the chart and clearly identifiable—in line. A fix from one transit and one (carefully-taken) bearing at nearly right angles to it should be quite accurate.

Often you can only see to identify one charted object. A bearing on this, while not giving a proper fix, can be a useful check against your EP. When making any kind of fix or EP note the time beside it on the chart.

Take great care to identify correctly any marks you are using for plotting your position, and the same goes for any mark you are heading for as a planned waypoint. In addition to the list of chart table instru-ments make sure you have a good pair of binoculars (7 × 50s are the favoured size) and for night-time

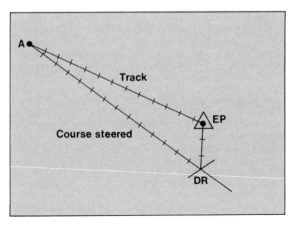

◆ Another type of tidal triangle, to calculate EP (estimated position) from DR (dead reckoning). DR is based simply on course steered, time and speed though the water. In this case you plot the direction of the tide from your DR and mark off the 'drift' (the distance you will have been pushed by the tide), which is the speed of the stream multiplied by the time in hours. The line from A to your EP (which you don't have to draw) represents course and distance made good.

Here we have a boat travelling for 2 hours at 7 knots through the water and a tidal drift of three miles (1½ knot stream); the tide is slightly against the boat and the distance made good is just over 12½ miles.

As with the other diagram, the dashes through the lines are shown only to explain the principle of marking off the units. Note that DR is shown as a simple stroke through the 'course steered' line, while EP is distinguished by a dot in a small triangle.

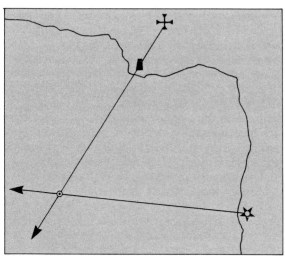

navigation a stopwatch is invaluable for identifying marks by the rhythm of their lights.

If visibility starts to decrease take whatever fix you can while there are objects still visible to take bearings of.

ECHO SOUNDER NAVIGATION

When following a coastline you may be more concerned to assess the distance from the shore than your exact position. If you know where you are along a coastline you can do this with your echo sounder. Work out the height of tide and subtract it from the depth indicated (your echo sounder should be adjusted to show depths of water, not depth under the transducer) to give chart datum. Note the results along a short length of your track then compare them with the figures on the chart.

An echo sounder can be a useful navigational tool, not just a device to warn you when you are about to run aground. Besides helping you work out distance off, it can be used in conjunction with a chart to tell you when you are passing over a noticeable trough or peak on the seabed. And you can use a sounding in conjunction with a position line gained from bearings or a transit to give you some idea of your position, if not actually to fix it.

ELECTRONIC NAVIGATION AIDS

Sophisticated navigational aids such as radar, Decca, Satnav and Loran C are really outside the scope of this book, in which we are concentrating on the

◖ ◄ The best possible fix is a navigation buoy with its name or number on it (left), but it is essential to check its identification carefully. Using a transit to obtain a fix (above) should be dead accurate as long as you have a good bearing and have identified the objects in line correctly.

basics of motor boating. No amount of electronic sophistication should let you forget the basic skills of navigation. Not only can electronics go haywire, or the necessary electrical power fail altogether, but even when using a Decca navigator in 'waypoint' mode (to tell you what course to steer, how far you

◄ A three-point fix, of a rather idealised kind, with three objects bearing roughly 120° apart. The resulting triangle is called a cocked hat, and if it is reasonably small you can assume that you are somewhere near the middle. By convention a fix is drawn on the chart as a dot in a circle. If there are only two identifiable objects on which to take bearings, the point at which the resulting lines cross is your fix—even if the lines are at 90° such a fix is not so reliable, but better than nothing.

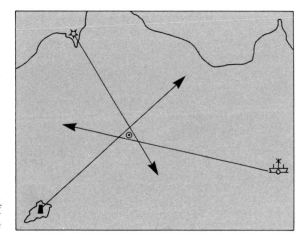

have to go, when you should arrive and how far off your track you are) you still need to practise many of those basic skills. You still have to read the chart and work out safe courses (and still try to use navigation marks as waypoints so you can keep a check on the electronic navigator's performance) and you should still record your position at regular intervals in the logbook. And although a black box will show you the effect of any tidal stream on your progress, which you can then counter, you will steer a straighter, more efficient course if you work out an allowance for tide beforehand.

To use radar properly, either for collision avoidance in bad visibility or as a navigation aid (in good or bad visibility), requires considerable skill and experience. But with that skill and experience it can be very useful indeed. Plotting with radar requires particular care because the picture you get may bear little relation to the actual shape of the coastline, but it can be good for measuring distance.

Before the advent of electronic navigators for pleasure craft and the reduction in size and price of radar, RDF (radio direction finding) was a widely used navigational aid. Many sailors still use it, but on motor boats, particularly fast motor boats, it is almost impossible to operate with any accuracy.

PILOTAGE

Where navigation—of the formal, plotting-courses-on-a-chart variety—ends and pilotage begins is a grey area. In pilotage you use many of the same techniques but also your powers of observation and common-sense deduction.

Pilotage is interpretation of charts and the natural and man-made features they show, and the application of local knowledge—your own or that passed on in a pilot book.

Pilotage is noting from the chart that, as you head in towards a harbour, you can avoid a nasty patch of shallow water by keeping the end of the harbour wall open to port of the rock with a beacon on it. A clearing line, as it's called, does not have to be between two objects; if there isn't a handy rock and beacon it could be a bearing, on the end of that harbour wall, above or below which it is safe to approach. But remember to make proper allowance for the tidal stream.

KEEPING A LOG

An essential element of navigation is the keeping of a clear record of every passage, as you go along. You can buy a nautical logbook in a chandlery, but you may find that the headings or the sizes of the columns don't suit you and it is easy enough to make up your own.

A well-kept logbook will also have notes on weather conditions and records of engine performance (as a means of keeping a watch on such things as oil pressure and cooling water temperature), fuelling and watering.

Date 17/10/87 Passage from Gillingham to Ramsgate
High water _Sheerness_ Time 0901 BST Height 4·3 m
Ramsgate Time 2034 BST Height 3·5 m
---------------- Time   Height

Time	Log	Location	Towards	Course steered	Speed	Weather	Engine(s) Water	Oil	Fuel	Water
0845	0	Gillingham Marina	Garrison Pt.	River channel	8	E 3/4 Fair	75	55	70gal 30gal at Gillingham
0958	7·8	Garrison Point	Medway 2 By	Medway channel	10	E 2/3 Fair	75	55	
1025	12·0	Medway 2 By	'F' Beacon	122°	10		78	55	
1035	13·5	'F' Beacon	Spile By	120°	10				
1050	15·9	Spile By	Spaniard By	099°	10				
1110	18·8	Middle Sand Bn in line with Red Sand Towers	"	"	10	E 1/2 Slight Haze			
1140	23·9	Spaniard By	E Last By	122°	10		78	55	

◆ **Suggested logbook format and entries for part of a cruise from the Medway to Ramsgate in southern England. You may wish to add other headings—but don't make your logbook so complicated that you or your crew are too daunted to fill it in.**

7 Watching the weather

Before you put to sea—before you even decide to put to sea—you should know what you are likely to face in the way of weather. That means more than just noting the predicted wind force and direction on the harbour office noticeboard, and more, even, than recording the synopsis, the area forecasts and the weather reports in the last radio shipping forecast.

Shipping forecasts are the best source of information, but to get a clear picture of what the weather is up to you need to listen to them for two or three days before any trip. You need also to learn the terminology used—exactly what does the meteorologist mean by such basic English words as 'soon' and 'rapidly'?

In addition to the shipping forecasts, coastal weather bulletins are available from a variety of sources, not so detailed but still very useful especially if you fail to stay awake for the late-night shipping forecast or fail to wake up for the early-morning one (both are broadcast at anti-social hours). Don't ignore the general forecasts on TV and in the newspapers; they may be thin on detail as far as winds go, but their weather charts are a good indicator of the type of weather to be expected.

Learn to supplement the information the forecasts give you with observations of the sky and of changes in pressure and temperature. And remember that weather predictions need to be translated into predictions of sea state, taking into account the direction of tidal streams and, in shallow water, the height of tide, and local factors such as sea and land breezes and the degree of shelter, if any.

Meteorology, as practised by meteorologists, is a sophisticated science. As practised by boating people it is a matter of listening to the forecasts, commonsense seamanship and local knowledge. But it certainly helps to have a basic understanding of what happens—if not why it happens—in the weather patterns that affect us.

HIGHS AND LOWS

The weather revolves around areas of high atmospheric pressure, called *anticyclones* or simply *highs*, and areas of low pressure, called *depressions* or *lows*. In the northern hemisphere the wind blows clockwise around a high and anti-clockwise around a low, and vice versa south of the equator.

◆ A grossly simplified weather pattern showing isobars around a depression, or low, and round an anticyclone, or high. Winds blow anti-clockwise round a depression and clockwise round an anticyclone, roughly parallel to the isobars but slightly inwards round a depression, slightly outwards round an anticyclone. The illustration shows a typical European weather scenario with a depression passing close to Iceland and a large anticyclone to the south, over the central Mediterranean. A south-westerly airstream covers most of northern Europe.

Weather maps show the contour lines of equal air pressure, called *isobars*, around lows and highs. The wind blows more or less parallel to the isobars, though angled slightly inwards towards a low and outwards from a high. The closer together the isobars, the stronger the winds. Think of a low pressure area (the source of more strong winds than a high) as a whirlpool: the water flows faster the steeper the slope of its sides. Round a low the wind blows harder the steeper the slope from high to low pressure.

In most parts of northern Europe, the prevailing wind is between westerly and south-westerly because depressions tend to pass to the north, anticyclones to the south. You can turn that around to remind yourself which way the wind goes round lows and highs. Generally speaking, low pressure is associated with bad weather, high pressure with good weather, but of course it is not as simple as that. For example, in certain conditions and at certain times of the year high pressure can bring fog, which is feared by many people more than gales. We will look at fog in due course.

FRONTS, TROUGHS AND RIDGES

You will notice, on any detailed weather map, lines radiating out from depressions, crossing the isobars where they (the isobars) make a sharp turn. These lines represent *fronts*, which are the boundaries between warm air masses and cold air masses. A *warm front*, in which warm air catches up with cold, is shown by a line with black or red semi-circles on its leading edge. A *cold front*, in which cold air catches up with warm, is shown by a line with black or blue triangles. Sometimes a cold front catches up with a warm front to produce what is called an *occluded front*, indicated on a weather map by alternate semi-circles and triangles.

The centre of a depression is rarely circular. Sometimes they become quite sausage-shaped and then they are known as troughs of low pressure, which can split into two depressions. Anticyclones are even more likely to be odd shapes. When they become elongated they are known as ridges of high pressure.

LOCAL WIND VARIATIONS

The strength of the wind, as mentioned, varies with the spacing of the isobars, and can be predicted with reasonable accuracy, at least on the open sea. But close to land the wind can be subject to a number of local effects like those that cause sea breezes. On hot summer afternoons the land heats up more quickly than the sea and the air over the land rises, drawing in the cooler air over the sea, and creating an onshore wind—the sea breeze. If the wind is already blowing onshore it will strengthen; if offshore it could weaken or even reverse direction. Land breezes occur at night and in the early morning; they are offshore winds caused by the air over the land cooling more quickly than the air over the sea. Other local variations include the funnelling of winds up and down estuaries and the deflection of wind around obstructions such as headlands.

If you go boating in the Mediterranean you should familiarise yourself with its many local winds. Most of them are offshore winds, from mountains or out of the major river valleys, and they can arrive suddenly and blow viciously for several days.

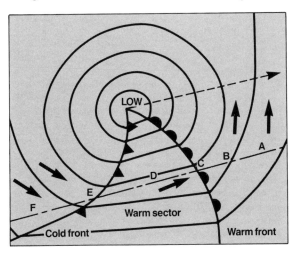

Cold front — Warm sector — Warm front

◄ **A boat on the line between A and F would experience the following weather as a low passes by:**

A. The approach of the depression would be signalled by a backing of the wind (here from SW to SSW), falling pressure and a build-up of cloud; streaky cirrus to start off with, then an overall cover of thin cirrostratus and light rain.

B. The wind strengthens and continues to back (towards the south), the pressure falls more rapidly, the cloud cover—of altostratus and then nimbostratus—becomes complete, and it begins to rain heavily.

C. As the warm front passes the wind veers (back to SW), the pressure stops falling and rain eases up or stops.

D. The warm sector gives low cloud and mist.

E. The passing of the cold front is marked by a sharp veering of the wind (to W or NW), rising pressure, the break-up of cloud and improved visibility. There may be some squalls, accompanied by showers.

F. Pressure rises further and the weather improves. Most of the clouds will be cumulus, but large cumulonimbus clouds may form giving strong squalls or thunderstorms.

← **Common cloud formations: Cirrus.**

← **Cirrostratus.**

← **Altostratus.**

← **Nimbostratus.**

WIND STRENGTH AND SEA STATE

The height of waves depends not just on the strength of the wind but on its fetch (the distance it has been blowing over open water) and the length of time it has been blowing. But it is not so much a high wave that is dangerous as a steep one, and especially the wave that breaks when it becomes too steep to support itself. On the open sea, in deep water, waves start to break in winds of over force 5, but as they approach shallow water they can steepen and break in lesser winds. When the tide is flowing in the opposite direction to the wind the sea is noticeably rougher; again, the effect is to steepen the waves and make life more uncomfortable.

The lesson to be learned from all of this is to avoid approaching an estuary with a shallow entrance in an onshore wind at any time other than just before high water.

One of the most uncomfortable and dangerous sea conditions is the convergence of waves from different directions. Besides the waves directly generated by the wind, others can hit you that have been refracted round a headland or that have bounced off a cliff or harbour wall. Ocean swells, created by storms hundreds of miles away and some days earlier, can also complicate things. When waves from different directions meet they will occasionally combine to form a wave of well above the average height or steepness.

FOG

Sea fog occurs when a mass of warm, humid air blows over a cold sea and is cooled below its dew point (the temperature at which the water in the air condenses). In north-west Europe it is air from the Azores and further south, blown on a prolonged south-

- Cumulus.
- Cumulonimbus.

WIND SPEEDS

Beaufort force	General description	Speed (knots)
0	Calm	Under 1
1	Light	1–3
2	Light	4–6
3	Light	7–10
4	Moderate	11–16
5	Fresh	17–21
6	Strong	22–27
7	Strong	28–33
8	Gale	34–40
9	Severe gale	41–47
10	Storm	48–55
11	Violent storm	56–63
12	Hurricane	64 and over

SPEEDS OF WEATHER SYSTEMS

Slowly	0–15 knots
Steadily	15–25 knots
Rather quickly	25–35 knots
Rapidly	35–45 knots
Very rapidly	Over 45 knots

TIMING OF GALE WARNINGS

Imminent	within 6 hours
Soon	6–12 hours
Later	12–24 hours

('Later' is also used about wind changes in forecasts)

westerly airstream, that is the chief culprit. Inshore, the sea is coldest and fog most common in winter and spring. In the summer and autumn fog banks can build up over the colder water offshore.

Fortunately, fog usually forms only in light airs. Once formed it can persist in winds up to force 4 or 5, but you rarely have to face both fog and heavy seas at the same time.

Along the coast you may encounter land or radiation fog that has formed overnight in cold, clear air. This type of fog usually disperses quite quickly when it drifts over the sea.

RECORDING FORECASTS

To understand forecasts fully you need to understand the terms used to describe the speeds (of wind and weather systems) and timing (of forecast gales and wind changes). A list of terms is given in the box above.

Shipping forecasts start with any gale warnings that are in force, and a general synopsis of the weather giving details of the movements of depressions, anticyclones, troughs of low pressure and ridges of high pressure. The sea area forecasts follow, with the expected wind direction and force, the weather ('fair', 'showers', etc) and the visibility. Finally there are the reports from coastal stations, giving wind speed and direction, weather, visibility, pressure and pressure trend ('falling', 'rising', 'rising slowly', etc).

Recording forecasts accurately requires practice. Develop some form of quick but neat shorthand (using a system of figures, initial letters, obliques and dashes) that you can understand, and preferably, one which the other members of your crew can make some sense of too.

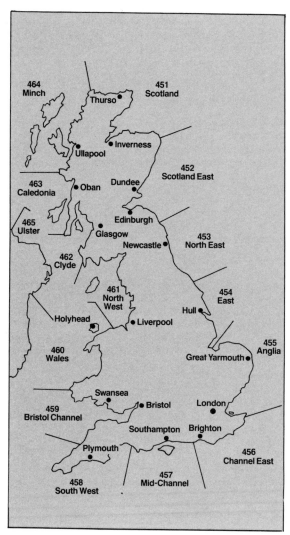

➤ Shipping forecast areas and the reporting coastal stations: T is Tiree, BL Butt of Lewis, Su Sumburgh, SAH St Abb's Head, Dow Dowsing, Dov Dover, RS Royal Sovereign, CLV Channel Light Vessel, Sc Scilly, V Valentia, R Ronaldsway, MH Malin Head, J Jersey

✦ Marinecall forecasts available by telephone. Ring 0898 500 followed by the 3-figure number of the area you want a forecast for. The forecasts are updated 2 or 3 times a day. For a 3- to 6-day outlook ring 0898 500 450.

If you are really serious about working out what the weather is going to be doing for the next 24 hours or more—if for instance you are making a long passage—you can plot your own weather map from the information the shipping forecast gives you. Use one of the pads of forecast sheets that you can buy (*Metmaps* published by the Meteorological Office and the Royal Yachting Association, for example). The techniques involved in drawing a weather map are well described in *Weather at Sea* by David Houghton, published by Fernhurst Books.

PERSONAL OBSERVATION

Careful study of the clouds can often give you a good idea of changes in the weather. Only with practice

and experience can you become reasonably proficient at 'reading' the sky, but the pictures and captions on pages 56–57, in conjunction with the diagram of a depression on page 55, offer some of the basic theory.

The humble barometer can also be a very useful aid to do-it-yourself forecasting. Take little notice of the quaint 'rain', 'change' and 'fair' signs. It is the change in pressure, or rather the rate of change of pressure, that is important. A rapid fall or rapid rise (more than three millibars either way in three or four hours) portends strong winds.

Wind shifts also give clues to weather changes. A backing wind (moving anti-clockwise in direction, eg from west to south-west) often means the approach of a depression, whereas a veering wind (moving clockwise) might mean the passing of a front and the approach of better weather.

MARINE FORECASTS BY RADIO, TV AND TELEPHONE

BBC Radio

Shipping forecasts. On Radio 4 on 198kHz LW and on various Radio 4 local MW frequencies at 00.33, 05.55, 13.55 and 17.50. All local times. *Coastal waters forecasts.* At 00.38 on Radio 4 on 198kHz LW and on various Radio 4 local MW frequencies, and on Radio Scotland on 810kHz. At 06.55 on Radio 3 on 1215kHz MW. Local times.
Gale warnings. On Radio 4 198kHz LW and MW frequencies, at the earliest opportunity (between programmes) after receipt and following the first news bulletin after receipt.

Radio Telefis Eirann

Irish coastal waters forecasts on RTE Radio 1 on 567 and 729kHz MW at 06.33 and 11.55 (12.10 on Sundays).

Local Radio

Many local radio stations in coastal areas broadcast coastal waters forecasts and also 'Small Craft Warnings' when winds of force 6 or more are forecast.

Teletext and Prestel

Oracle (ITV) teletext shows the shipping forecast (updated three times a day). Prestel phone-linked TV information service shows detailed weather information, including shipping forecasts.

Marinecall

Telephone forecast service. See opposite page.

Coast radio stations

Forecasts on VHF (radiotelephones) are broadcast by UK coast radio stations at 08.03 and 20.03 or 08.33 or 20.33 depending on the station (all times are GMT), on a working channel after an announcement on Ch 16. Also, forecasts are available on request; call the nearest coast radio station on one of its working channels .

HM Coastguard (VHF)

Coastguard Maritime Rescue Co-ordination Centres and Sub-Centres broadcast forecasts on VHF Ch 67 (after an announcement on Ch 16) at four-hourly intervals, or two-hourly intervals if strong winds are forecast. The first forecast is broadcast at the following times: Moray 00.10, Aberdeen 03.20, Forth 02.05, Tyne/Tees 01.50, Humber 03.40, Great Yarmouth 00.40, Thames 02.50, Dover 01.05, Solent 00.40, Portland 02.20, Brixham 00.50, Falmouth 01.40, Hartland 01.20, Ramsay 03.50, Belfast 03.05, Clyde 00.20, Oban 02.40, Stornoway 01.10, Pentland 01.35, Shetland 01.05.

Navtex

By installing the appropriate receiver you can obtain printed-out forecasts and other information from various coast radio stations in NW Europe.

Weather facsimile

Weather charts transmitted by radio can be printed out using a weather facsimile receiver.

8 VHF radio

A VHF radiotelephone is probably the most popular item of marine equipment after the compass, the echo sounder and lifejackets. Boat owners buy VHF as a safety aid as much as for the convenience of talking to their friends on other boats, or making link phone calls, or calling up the marina to book a berth. And while the Mayday call is one that every skipper hopes never will have to be made, it's reassuring to know that, in coastal waters at least, a radio Mayday is the surest and quickest way to alert the rescue services.

TYPES OF VHF

With several good, handheld, pocket-size sets available at affordable prices, it is feasible to use VHF on the very smallest of boats. However, if you can install a fixed set and aerial you will have the benefit of greater power, at not necessarily greater cost. Most fixed sets can be operated on either 25 watts or one watt (the 1W setting is mandatory) while the maximum power on handhelds is usually between one and five watts.

The maximum range of any VHF set is restricted to a little more than 'line of sight' between calling and receiving stations: from your aerial (at about its middle) to just over the horizon, plus an equivalent figure for whoever you are talking to. So the maximum range between two boats with good aerials (the quality of the aerials is as important as the height) will be about 12 to 20 miles. Between a boat and the high aerials of a coast radio station or Coastguard rescue centre it, could, in theory, be 80 miles or more but in practice is between about 30 and 50 miles. The maximum range of most handheld sets is limited by the low altitude of their aerials to between three and ten miles.

Most modern fixed sets, and many handheld sets, can operate on any of the 57 international channels and a limited number of private channels, including Channel M, the one for booking that marina berth. Many sets have a useful function called dual watch, on which you can listen out on Channel 16, the distress and calling channel, and any one other. If there's any traffic on either channel the set will automatically lock on to it.

VHF CHANNELS AND THEIR USES

Channel 16 is the lynchpin, the 'Distress, Safety and Calling' channel. With a number of exceptions— when calling a coast radio station, a marina radio and, usually, a port radio—you first make contact on Ch 16 before switching to a working channel. Ch 16 should be kept as clear as possible for emergency traffic; it should never be used to pass messages, except in an emergency.

By prior arrangement you can call another boat on a working channel, but you should generally be monitoring Ch 16. The table on this page shows the allocated uses of different channels.

MAIN VHF CHANNEL ALLOCATIONS

Distress, Safety and Calling
16.

Inter-ship
06, 08, 72, 77.

Port operations (see nautical almanacs for specific port radio channels; note that some should be called on their working channels, others on Ch 16)
12, 14, 11, 68.

Public correspondence (see nautical almanacs for specific coast radio station working channel; call on vacant working channel)
26, 27, 25, 24, 23, 28, 04, 01, 03, 02, 05, 87, 86, 83, 85.

Small Craft Safety (non-emergency calls between Coastguard and pleasure craft; calling on Ch 16) (UK only)
67.

Marinas (also some yacht clubs) (UK only)
M (sometimes referred to as 37).

↞ Handheld radios like this one have a limited range, but bring the advantages of VHF to even the smallest boat. They are useful as spare sets on larger craft too.

RADIO PROCEDURE

Before you press the transmit button you must do two things: work out what you are going to say—to keep your transmission to a minimum and to save yourself the embarrassment of a public display of um-ing and er-ing—and check that there's no-one already speaking on the channel you are going to use. Always say the name of the station you are calling first. Your first message need be no more complicated than:

'SKYLARK, THIS IS PUFFIN. OVER.'

There is no need to repeat either of the names, nor to add 'Do you read me?' or 'Come in please'. Release the transmit button as soon as you have said 'over'. *Skylark* should acknowledge the call in similar vein and, assuming the initial call was on Ch 16, should suggest a channel on which to work, in this case obviously one of the inter-ship channels:

'PUFFIN, THIS IS SKYLARK, CHANNEL SIX, OVER.'

Before switching to Ch 6 *Puffin* should acknowledge the suggestion, by saying simply:

'CHANNEL SIX'.

VHF AND THE LAW

Any boat owned and based in the UK and fitted with VHF must have a Ship Licence issued by the Department of Trade and Industry, Room 613(c), Waterloo Bridge House, Waterloo Road, London SE1 8UA. When you receive the licence, which is renewable annually, you will also receive a call sign of four letters, possibly prefixed by a single-digit number. You may licence a portable set in the same way but you can then only use it on the boat for which it is licenced. The alternative is to take out a Transportable Licence, but with this you won't receive a call sign and cannot make link phone calls.

To use a VHF on a boat the skipper, or at least one member of the crew, must have a radio operator's certificate. This is usually the 'Certificate of Competence, Restricted VHF Only', for which you need to pass a simple test—simple if you know the basic rules of radio procedure and the phonetic alphabet. The certificate is issued by the Royal Yachting Association; tests are held at a number of nautical colleges, adult education institutes and some yacht clubs. Further details from the RYA, RYA House, Romsey Road, Eastleigh, Hants SO5 4YA.

The law also has quite a lot to say about the use of VHF. For example, when in harbour you are not allowed to communicate with other vessels, except on safety matters. You may not pass messages ashore (other than to shore stations such as port radios) except through a coast radio station. You are not allowed to transmit 'unnecessary or superfluous signals'. You must not divulge the contents of any messages you overhear on the radio. You must not use profane, indecent or obscene language.

▲ **Using a fixed radio with a telephone-type handset, the operator is establishing contact on Channel 16 before switching to a working channel.**

Then, after switching to Ch 6 and checking that it's clear *Puffin* calls *Skylark* again and passes her message. Thereafter, the conversation can continue normally, but keeping it brief and remembering to say 'OVER' each time you want the other boat to reply. When *Skylark*, say, wants to end the conversation, she says:

'OUT.' (Not 'Over and out', which is a contradiction in terms.)

Both boats should then switch back to monitoring Ch 16.

Whenever you need to spell a word use the phonetic alphabet (see this page). When giving your call sign always spell it out phonetically; it's a good idea to have it displayed on the set. As further aids to understanding and brevity certain words, called 'prowords', have been adopted and should be learnt, and used when appropriate. For example, if you have made a mistake and want to correct it don't ·waffle away with apologies and explanations, just say CORRECTION and give the corrected message. ACKNOWLEDGE means 'Have you received and understood?'. CONFIRM means 'Is that correct?' (with your version of a message received that you wish to check). SAY AGAIN means 'Please repeat that message'. I SAY AGAIN means 'I will repeat that' (of important words and phrases). I SPELL means 'What follows is spelt phonetically'. RECEIVED means 'I acknowledge receipt' (of a message received and understood). STATION CALLING is used when answering a call from a station whose name has not been clearly heard.

When calling another station that is close to you, always ensure that your set is switched to 1W operation. For link calls and emergencies switch to 25W (or on handheld radios, whatever is the highest setting). If the station you are calling fails to answer, wait a couple of minutes before trying again, and then give up, at least until you are nearer and have a better chance of being heard.

CALLING THE COASTGUARD

As described in the chapter on weather, the Coastguard broadcasts four-hourly weather forecasts on Ch 67, after an announcement on Ch 16. You should make every effort to listen in to a broadcast weather forecast by this or other means, and not take the lazy way out of calling the Coastguard for a forecast when you want it.

The same goes for information about navigation and tides. Do your own homework. However, the Coastguard is there to help and if you have a genuine problem (short of an emergency—we will come on to emergency radio procedure shortly) call the nearest Coastguard Rescue Centre on Ch 16. You are likely to be asked to switch to Ch 67, the Small Craft Safety Channel.

When cruising out of your own area you can call the nearest Rescue Centre and give them your destination and estimated time of arrival. If you get into trouble this could help the rescue services, which are controlled by the Coastguard, to find you. But when you

▲ A coastguard using VHF to broadcast details of shipping movements in the Dover Straits. Coastguards also broadcast weather forecasts on Ch 67 every four hours.

arrive safely, or if you change your plans, you must let the Coastguard know, to forestall an unnecessary search.

COAST RADIO STATIONS

Link calls—linking your radio with the telephone network—can be made through the nearest coast radio station. Always make the initial call on one of the station's (unoccupied) working channels, giving your call sign and stating straight away that you want to make a link call:

'HUMBER RADIO, THIS IS SKYLARK, MIKE OSCAR ECHO ROMEO. LINK CALL PLEASE, OVER.'

The CRS will call back, instructing you to stand by, perhaps on a different channel (say you called on Ch 24 and are asked to switch to Ch 85). Acknowledge:

'HUMBER RADIO, THIS IS SKYLARK, CHANNEL EIGHT FIVE, OVER.'

There are two ways of paying for link calls. You can simply quote your AAIC (Accounting Authority Indicator Code), which for British boats is GB14 followed by your call sign, and you will be sent a bill for the call. Or, to use the cheaper YTD (yacht telephone debit) system, available to British yachts when calling a British phone number through a British CRS, preface the number you want to ring with 'YTD' (phonetically), followed by your home phone

number. When the station calls you back and asks what number you want, make it clear how you wish to pay. Either:

'HUMBER RADIO, THIS IS SKYLARK. GOLF BRAVO ONE FOUR. MIKE OSCAR ECHO ROMEO. (The number you want). OVER.'

or:

'HUMBER RADIO, THIS IS SKYLARK. YANKEE TANGO DELTA. (Your home phone number). LINK CALL TO (the number you want). OVER.'

When you finally get through remember that you are still operating in 'simplex' mode (unless you have an expensive, twin-aerial, 'duplex' VHF) so you must alternate your messages and say 'Over' to get a reply. Make this clear to the person you are talking to if he or she doesn't realise.

You can also receive calls through a CRS. The caller must ring the nearest CRS or dial 100 and ask for 'Ships Telephone Service' and give the name of the nearest CRS; or if that's not known, the location of the boat. Your boat's name will be mentioned in the next of the CRS's periodic 'Traffic list' broadcasts, unless you have Selcall, a device through which a CRS can send a coded signal to trigger an audio and visual alarm to tell you that there's a call for you.

If you are cruising out of your normal area and wish to ensure that anyone trying to call you finds you, contact your nearest CRS—and other CRSs whose area of coverage you pass through—and give them details of your position, destination and ETA. This system of CRSs keeping tabs on your whereabouts is known as TR ('traffic routeing'). When you have made contact with the CRS preface your message with 'TANGO ROMEO'. If you have asked for a TR you must tell the appropriate CRS that you have arrived at your destination.

Coast radio stations also broadcast useful information on VHF, including gale warnings, forecasts and navigational warnings.

EMERGENCY RADIO PROCEDURE

There are two types of emergency radio traffic: distress (Mayday) which takes priority over any other traffic, and urgency (Pan Pan), which takes priority over everything but distress traffic.

There is some confusion as to exactly what qualifies as distress. According to the International Telegraphic Union, which regulates radio usage, a distress message can only be made if *a vessel* is in immediate danger, but the International Maritime Organisation, which lays down the laws of the sea, has declared that a *vessel or person* being in immediate danger constitutes a distress situation. If you follow the ITU rules to the letter you can put out only a Pan Pan call if you have lost someone overboard or if someone aboard is dangerously ill, but it is now generally accepted that you can, in such circumstances, put out a Mayday call. A Pan Pan call should be made if, for example, you lose steerage or run out of fuel and there are no boats nearby that you can summon to your aid.

To send a distress or urgency message make sure you are switched to Ch 16 and on maximum power. Before pressing the transmit button pause for a second or two (however panic-stricken you are) to consider what you are going to say. The following is a (fictional) example of a distress message:

'MAYDAY MAYDAY MAYDAY
'THIS IS SKYLARK, SKYLARK
'MAYDAY, SKYLARK
'MY POSITION IS TWO MILES NORTH EAST OF SPURN POINT
'ENGINE-ROOM FIRE SPREADING AND OUT OF CONTROL
'REQUEST RESCUE AND MEDICAL AID
'FOUR PEOPLE ON BOARD, ONE BADLY BURNT
'OVER.'

...and an urgency message:

'PAN PAN, PAN PAN, PAN PAN
'ALL STATIONS
'THIS IS PUFFIN, PUFFIN
'MY POSITION IS THREE THREE ZERO DEGREES ONE MILE FROM HARTLAND POINT
'RUDDERS FOULED, HAVE LOST STEERAGE
'REQUEST ASSISTANCE
'OVER.'

If you have a Decca navigator, and it's still working, you can give your position as a latitude and longitude instead of a distance and bearing from an object.

If you hear a distress or urgency message do not answer it immediately. Give the Coastguard, or some other station better equipped to arrange help (like a coast radio station or a port radio), a few seconds to answer. However, if you hear no reply then acknowledge the message yourself:

'MAYDAY
'SKYLARK
'THIS IS MALLARD
'RECEIVED MAYDAY.'

Don't add 'Over', which would invite an answer. If you are able to, you must go to the aid of the boat in distress. You should also try relaying the distress message in the hope that a Coastguard rescue centre or other stations that couldn't hear the original distress message can hear you. A Mayday relay would run as follows:

'MAYDAY RELAY, MAYDAY RELAY, MAYDAY RELAY
'THIS IS MALLARD, MALLARD
'MAYDAY, SKYLARK
'POSITION TWO MILES NORTH EAST OF SPURN POINT
'ENGINE-ROOM FIRE SPREADING AND OUT OF CONTROL
'RESCUE AND MEDICAL AID REQUESTED
'FOUR PEOPLE ON BOARD, ONE BADLY BURNT
'OVER.'

Needless to say you should not use Ch 16 for any other traffic while you know that there's an emergency. The station controlling traffic—probably the nearest Coastguard rescue centre—may impose radio silence with the instruction 'SEELONCE MAYDAY', relaxing it (allowing restricted, essential traffic) in due course with 'PRUDENCE MAYDAY', and ending it with 'SEELONCE FEENEE'.

Make sure that everyone on board is capable of using the VHF, at least to make a Mayday call. Your life may depend on it.

DISTRESS MESSAGE

(Broadcast only when you are in serious and imminent danger and require immediate assistance.)

Select Channel 16

Press transmit button

'MAYDAY MAYDAY MAYDAY.

'THIS IS (boat's name, three times).

'MAYDAY (boat's name).

'MY POSITION IS (position as bearing **from** and distance from a known point, or latitude and longitude).

'(Nature of distress, eg fire, sinking).

'(Aid required).

'(Number of people on board).

'OVER.'

Release transmit button.

URGENCY MESSAGE

(Broadcast only when you require urgent assistance but are not in immediate danger.

Select Channel 16

Press transmit button

'PAN PAN, PAN PAN, PAN PAN.

'ALL STATIONS.

'THIS IS (boat's name, three times).

'MY POSITION IS (position as bearing **from** and distance from a known point, or latitude and longitude).

'(Nature of emergency).

'(Aid required).

'OVER.'

Release transmit button.

9 Passage making

Two of the essential ingredients of successful boating are careful planning and good seamanship; seamanship in the sense of knowing how not to get into trouble, but also knowing how to get out of it.

The following thoughts on planning and seamanship are geared to a longish coastal passage or short sea crossing, but much of it is just as applicable to an afternoon trip round the bay.

PASSAGE PLANNING

In a motor boat the most important factor in planning a passage of any length is fuel: how far you can safely travel without refuelling and where you can refuel. Keep well within your maximum range (see the panel opposite). Check up from the pilot books and almanacs that you will be able to refuel where you want to—if in any doubt make your own enquiries.

At the same time find out all you can about the harbours and anchorages you plan to visit, and about those that might be suitable 'bolt holes' if the weather or anything else forces you to seek shelter before you reach your destination. In particular you need to know about any tidal or weather restrictions on entry and exit, and where visiting boats berth.

We looked at the navigation aspect of planning in Chapter 6. When plotting your courses and calculating your distances work out your timing as well. You want to time your departure to make the most of the tidal streams—especially in a slow boat—and, maybe, so as to arrive at your destination at a certain time. If entry there is restricted to, say, two hours either side of high water you want to aim to arrive in the early part of that period, to give yourself a margin for delay. Also, you want to complete every passage in daylight—especially in a fast boat, to which unsighted driftwood and other floating objects can pose a serious threat. If the timing doesn't work you will have to amend your plan, or go on another day when the times of high water are more convenient.

WATCHKEEPING

On a long passage, share out the various chores that need doing and rotate the essential jobs of steering and keeping a look-out. There's no need for the skipper to impose a rigid, naval-style watchkeeping rota, but depending on the number of crew each

➤ **Floating debris can punch a hole in the hull of a fast boat, so make fast passages by day to reduce the risk.**

could do, say, one hour on and two hours off, preferably with at least two people 'on duty' at any time, steering and helping to keep a look-out. It's vital in a fast motor boat to keep a keen look-out for objects floating in the water ahead.

A good skipper will maintain the interest of the crew by delegating as many jobs as possible; keeping the log up to date, recording the DR (dead reckoning) at regular intervals, taking fixes, recording weather forecasts.

KEEPING WARM, DRY AND WELL FED

Even in mid-summer you must be prepared for the weather to be wet and cold. Take warm and windproof trousers and sweaters and waterproof (not just showerproof) jacket and trousers. Wear shoes with good non-slip soles or, in the wet, a pair of seaboots, again with effective non-slip soles. A change of clothes, even on the shortest day trip, is a sensible precaution.

The prime requirement of food eaten on passage is that it be easy to prepare, preferably requiring nothing more than heating up. If the weather's cold something hot will be appreciated, even if it's just soup. There's much to be said for breaking up a long passage with regular snacks and hot drinks. Even if you usually scorn it, some form of chocolate is a good restorer of morale and energy.

Warmth and food (or more specifically some kind of liquid refreshment) are particularly important to anyone suffering from seasickness; don't allow a seasick person to start suffering from hypothermia and dehydration as well. As far as preventing seasickness is concerned there's a variety of patent preventatives available. If you are a sufferer try them out to discover the best one for you; some people find that certain types have the side-effect of inducing drowsiness. Fresh air can be one of the most effective cures if you start to feel sick when you are in an enclosed wheelhouse or down below.

ROUGH SEAS

The best thing to do with bad weather is to avoid it, to stay in harbour or make harbour before its onset. In a motor boat, even in a slow displacement motor boat, you should usually be able to avoid strong winds and dangerous sea conditions, by careful recording of forecasts and cautious planning. Always be prepared to curtail your plans and postpone leaving harbour,

even if that means getting back a day late from a cruise or having to leave your boat somewhere and collecting her at a later date.

However cautious you are, if you use your boat extensively you will one day find yourself at sea in conditions that you would rather have sat out in harbour. When this happens you have to decide whether to carry on along your planned route, probably at reduced speed, or alter course to seek shelter.

In considering the first option take into account your fuel reserves and your fuel consumption, in

KNOW YOUR RANGE

Most boatbuilders give honest and reasonably accurate information on fuel consumption and the maximum range of their boats, but remember that such figures usually apply to new boats without all the equipment and gear that will be carried aboard when cruising, and with a weed-free bottom. You can and should make your own calculations as well.

First check your speed against different rpm on a measured mile—speedos can be, and often are, inaccurate. Do one run each way on each setting, to nullify the effect of any tidal stream. You can then work out your range based on the quoted fuel consumption per hour at various rpm settings, which should be fairly accurate. Divide your tank capacity (gallons or litres) by your consumption (gallons or litres per hour) to give your maximum *theoretical* range in hours. Multiply by the speed (knots) to give your maximum *theoretical* range in nautical miles. Subtract at least 10 per cent so that you never get down to the bottom of the tank and risk sediment being sucked into the engine. Subtract another 10 to 15 per cent to allow for unintentional or enforced detours, bad weather (punching into head seas will increase your consumption) and any minor miscalculations you have made in estimating your consumption.

Then take every opportunity to check up on your fuel consumption: for example fill up your tanks before you undertake any long passages and see how much is required to refill them. If the weather conditions have allowed you to maintain a fairly constant rpm you will get an accurate idea of your consumption. Keep a record of your calculations.

terms of gallons (or litres) per hour rather than miles per gallon (or litre)—you will start to burn more fuel per mile in rough seas, especially if you are punching into them. Work out how the situation is going to develop. Will you soon be in more sheltered, or less sheltered, water? Is the tide about to turn and, if so, will the sea get worse (wind against tide) or better (wind over tide)?

Before you turn and head towards the nearest harbour consider what conditions will be like as you approach the shore. If it's a lee shore (the wind blowing on to it) the seas will become steeper and more dangerous as they enter shallow water, and a lee shore is no place to be caught if, for example, you suffer an engine breakdown. Work out what the state of the tide will be when you arrive off the harbour and check with your almanac and pilot book on any tidal restrictions—although, as suggested earlier, you should have already made a note of them.

All loose items of equipment, above and below decks, should be secured as soon as the going gets rough. Lifejackets should be worn when working on deck in all but the calmest conditions. When

◄ **A heavy, confused sea like this calls for 100 percent concentration in driving the boat, while not forgetting the equally important task of keeping a look-out for other vessels and floating debris. The most comfortable and safest course will usually be with the waves just off the bow.**

things get really hairy they should be donned by everyone, whether on deck (where you shouldn't go unless you have to), in the cockpit or down below. Make sure all windows and adjustable ventilators are firmly closed. Check the bilges regularly and pump them out when necessary.

Reduce speed enough to make life on board reasonably comfortable but not so much as to lose steerage. How rough it has to be for a fast boat to come off the plane will depend on the design of the boat and on the direction she's going relative to the waves. Many boats slam intolerably in quite moderate head seas; others plough into the waves quite smoothly, though they may be very wet. Many become uncontrollable in following seas, trying their best to broach (turn beam on to the waves); others hold their course well. Some displacement boats can also be very difficult to handle in following seas.

A big sea on the beam (sideways on) is generally the most dangerous. Most boats are best handled in rough seas by keeping the waves just off the bow. If necessary you can make to windward by steering with the waves on the port bow for a while, then on the starboard bow, like tacking in a sailing boat.

ADJUSTING YOUR TRIM

Many fast motor boats have adjustable trim tabs on the stern, or power trim on outboard engines or out-drive legs. With these you can alter the running angle of your boat to suit different conditions. Depress the trim tabs and you lift the stern and lower the bow; raise the tabs for the opposite effect. Angle your outboard or outdrive leg outwards and your bow will rise; angle it in and your bow will drop.

Adjust your trim tabs or power trim as necessary to give you a ride that is both efficient (watch your speedometer) and comfortable. In a head sea it is generally best to ride reasonably level to reduce slamming, but don't lower the bow so much that the boat starts kicking up excessive spray or is in danger of shipping 'solid' water. In a following sea you may need to adopt a bows-up attitude to stop the boat digging into waves and maybe broaching.

FOG

Bad visibility can be just as frightening as rough seas and again should be avoided if at all possible. Rule number one is to slow down, to give yourself a chance of avoiding anything that might suddenly appear ahead, if necessary by stopping.

If possible take a fix from whatever landmarks or seamarks are in sight before the fog becomes too thick. If you are steering towards a mark note the compass course you are on before the mark vanishes from sight. Hoist your radar reflector, if it's not per-manently hoisted, and switch on your radar, if you have one. Remember that in fog—when the visibility is less than 1000 metres—you must sound the appro-priate fog signal, which for a motor boat under way is one long blast at least every two minutes.

Keep a keen look-out, and a keen listen-out for the sound of other vessels' fog signals and engines. In boats with partially or completely enclosed wheel-houses at least one member of the crew should be outside to improve your chances of seeing or hearing anything. In shallow water keep a watch on your echo sounder too.

◆ Using the trim tabs, or the power trim on an outboard or outdrive engine, you can adjust the angle of the boat to run either level or with bows up to suit the sea state.

If you're in a shipping channel get out of it as quickly as you can, so long as there is sufficient depth of water for your boat. Wherever you are, accurate navigation and steering become even more important than usual.

BOATING IN THE DARK

Some cruising yachtsmen claim to prefer making passages by night, arguing that navigation marks and shipping are best identified by their lights. But without considerable experience boating at night can be an anxious business. Distance can be difficult to judge and there's the constant worry about unlit marks and hazards. Above all, there's the increased danger of hitting something floating on or just under the surface. Fast boats should avoid night passages altogether, and fortunately they are the ones most able to do so.

If you are at sea at night, make sure you are showing the right lights (see Chapter 4). Have the necessary charts, plotting aids and books ready to hand. Turn off all the lights that might impair the helmsman's night vision; arrange the light over the chart table (preferably a directional light on a flexible lead) so that it doesn't shine in his or her eyes.

When making a long passage at night, time your arrival, if possible, for just after dawn. This will give you the benefit of navigation mark lights to make your landfall but allow you to enter harbour and moor in daylight.

ENGINE CHECKS

Keep a regular check on whatever engine gauges you have fitted, most commonly cooling water temperature, oil pressure and battery charging (ammeter and/or voltmeter). You should know, from your engine manual and from experience, what temperature your engines should not exceed and what pressure your lubricating oil should not drop below. Your ammeter is likely to show a fairly significant positive reading at the beginning of a passage, decreasing as

the batteries are charged. It should not, at any time, show a negative charge. A voltmeter will register a reading of a little over the voltage system of your boat—between about 13V and 15V on a 12V system.

A sudden rise in temperature usually indicates a blockage in the cooling water system (most boat engines are water-cooled). A drop in oil pressure could indicate an oil leak, a defective oil pump or damaged bearings. In any case you should stop the engine immediately.

Look at your fuel gauge regularly as well, not so much for an accurate assessment of how much you have left (most fuel gauges are not very accurate) but to check that you haven't seriously miscalculated your fuel consumption, or that a fuel leak isn't rapidly draining your tank(s).

Don't rely on your instruments. Have a look over the engine(s) at regular intervals, at the same time perhaps as checking that there's no water in the bilges, and check for any obvious signs of trouble, like oil or water leaks. Look at the stern gland too. Check that it's not leaking, or at least, not leaking too much—two or three drips a minute is quite normal. If it's very hot and not letting in any water at all it is probably too tight.

GOING FOREIGN

When cruising to a foreign country you must comply with the Customs formalities both of the country you are visiting—precise details can be obtained through its tourist board offices—and of your home country.

Most countries require boats entering their waters to fly the yellow 'Q' flag, requesting Customs clearance, and to report to the nearest Customs office on arrival. Notable exceptions are France and Holland, which only expect to see a 'Q' flag if dutiable goods are being carried.

Some countries require the skippers of visiting boats to have some kind of certificate proving their ability to handle their boats. For British boat owners an appropriate Royal Yachting Association Certificate will be acceptable, or a form called the Certificate of Competence, available from the RYA, which must be endorsed by the secretary or a flag officer of an RYA-affiliated club, or by the principal of an RYA-approved training establishment.

All boats cruising to foreign parts should be registered (for British boats either under 'full registration' through the Registrar of Shipping or under the ultra-simplified Small Ships Register operated by the RYA) and should carry their registration certificates on board. Evidence of insurance, including third party, should also be carried, perhaps in the form of photocopies of insurance policies. And, of course, everyone on board should have a passport. Always fly a courtesy flag (a small version of the visited country's ensign).

'Temporary importation', free of any duty or tax, is commonly for either six months or a year, depending on the country. It may be possible to leave a boat in a country for longer if it is sealed by the Customs for a period.

In many countries the use of a foreign boat for anything other than private pleasure (eg for chartering) is strictly forbidden and some countries insist that the owner be on board whenever the boat is under way.

British boats must notify HM Customs before leaving British waters, by completing Form C1328, copies of which are available from Customs offices and from many marinas and clubs. Part I should be delivered or posted to the Customs office nearest to your port of departure. On returning from abroad (including the Channel Islands) fly your 'Q' flag and notify the Customs, either in person or by phone. If you have any dutiable goods on board you must complete Parts II and III of Form C1328 and await the arrival of a Customs Officer. If you have nothing to declare and cannot make contact with the Customs, you can notify your arrival by posting Part II of Form C1328.

Finally, remember the UK's strict anti-rabies rules forbidding the landing of animals from any boats arriving from overseas.

EMERGENCIES

Engine breakdown

Rescue statistics show that engine breakdown is the commonest cause of motor boats getting into trouble. And the commonest cause of breakdown is fuel starvation—fuel not getting to the engine either because there isn't any left in the tank(s) or because it's contaminated by dirt or water.

Dirt or water in the fuel is more likely to lead to reduced or surging revs than a sudden stoppage, and should be curable with a change of filter or draining of the water trap. With diesel engines the same symptoms could mean that air is being drawn into the system somewhere. If you do any work on a diesel engine that involves interrupting the fuel flow you will have to 'bleed' the engine's fuel system before restarting it. More on this and other engine topics in Chapter 10.

Man overboard

Happily the danger of losing someone overboard is far less in a motor boat than in a sailing boat, for the simple reason that there's not the same need to go up on deck regularly. But it can still happen, and when it does you should know what to do.

If the person steering sees the incident he should immediately turn the boat so the stern swings away from the casualty. Whoever sees it happening should shout 'Man overboard' and throw a lifebuoy towards the casualty. One person should have the sole job of

← A partially-deflated inflatable can be useful in helping to recover someone who has fallen overboard, particularly if the casualty is weakened or unconscious.

YACHT AND BOAT SAFETY SCHEME

By taking part in HM Coastguard's Yacht and Boat Safety Scheme you could improve your chances of being found if the worst should happen and you have to call upon the rescue services, whether you are on passage or boating in your local waters. The scheme is free and entails, in the first place, getting hold of a CG66 post-paid card from your nearest Coastguard station or from your marina or harbour office. Fill it in with the requested information about your boat and post it to your local Coastguard rescue centre.

Then, when you set out on a passage along the coast, you can inform the Coastguard rescue centre, either just before you set out or by VHF from the boat. Give your destination, estimated time of arrival and mention that your boat has a Safety Scheme card (and which rescue centre, if different, holds it). It's vital that you also contact the Coastguard when you arrive or if you change your plans and are going, or have gone, somewhere else.

You don't have to be in the Safety Scheme to call up the Coastguard and report your movements, but it is helpful. The card you fill in has a tear-off section that you can give to relatives or friends, who can then call your local rescue centre if they are worried about you.

keeping an eye on the casualty and directing the helmsman towards him.

When coming alongside someone in the water be very careful to keep your propeller(s) well away from him. Make sure you slip into neutral as soon as you are alongside.

Hauling someone out of the water can be very difficult indeed. The first thing to do is to get a rope round the casualty. If you have a bathing ladder, and if the casualty is still conscious, he may, with a helping hand or two, get himself out of the water. Otherwise it may just be a matter of hauling him as hard as you can, perhaps gaining some purchase by passing a line, or lines, round the casualty from a strongpoint on the boat. A dinghy, especially a partly-deflated inflatable, may be a useful stepping stone.

If you lose someone overboard without actually seeing him go over the side, retrace your steps by steering a reciprocal course. If you have VHF, put out a Mayday call (as described in Chapter 8), unless you sight the casualty immediately.

Underwater damage

This is another rare occurrence, but motor boats are occasionally holed, usually by hitting driftwood. Quick thinking and quick action is called for. Do what you can to stop up the hole, using whatever's to hand, preferably something solid but wrapped in cloth. Get pumping with electric and manual pumps, and buckets too.

A more likely event is the ensnaring of a propeller with rope or plastic sheet, a situation which could, like engine breakdown, become an emergency if not quickly sorted out. On inboard-powered boats—excepting those very few that have inspection hatches over the propellers—clearing a propeller at sea is no joke. Sometimes, but not very often, going astern will clear a prop. Otherwise the best method is to saw off the offending object with a sharp serrated knife strapped to a boat-hook, leaning over the side if you can reach, or from a dinghy if you can't. Going into the water to untangle the propeller should be a last resort, only to be attempted by an experienced swimmer, preferably clad in a wetsuit and with a facemask.

Fire

The types of fire extinguisher a boat should carry were described in Chapter 2. You can use water as well except on electrical fires or on burning liquids, such as cooking fat and petrol. On cooking fat fires a fire blanket is usually the best remedy, but use a fire extinguisher if that fails.

When using fire extinguishers aim at the base of a fire for best effect. Be prepared, when using a dry powder extinguisher (the best general-purpose type of extinguisher) for the resulting clouds of dense (but non-toxic) smoke. Engine-room extinguishants such as BCF can be dangerous while still concentrated in a confined space.

Clearly, prevention is better than cure; a fire can be disastrous even if you manage to put it out. Be extra careful about gas and petrol, always switching off your gas at the cylinder (which should be in a locker out on deck or in the cockpit with a direct overboard drain hole) after use. Check for gas leaks and petrol fumes every time you go on board, with a detector if one is fitted, or by having a good sniff round. Remember that gas is heavier than air and will collect low down in the boat. If gas or petrol fumes are detected, ventilate the boat by opening all windows and ports and pump the fumes out, using manual pumps and buckets—the embarrassment of apparently baling out nothing is preferable to the disaster of a fire or an explosion. Don't switch on the engines or anything electrical (including electric bilge pumps) until you are sure the gas or fumes have been cleared and until their source has been found and fixed.

Injury and illness

You are a long way from medical help on a boat. Everyone who goes boating regularly, whether as a skipper or crew, should learn at least the rudiments of first aid, and every boat should have a good first aid kit. Buy a book on first aid and keep it with the kit. You can obtain medical advice by VHF; call the nearest coast radio station, add the word Medico after your boat's name and you will be connected to a hospital. Make it a Pan Pan call if the situation is serious.

Calling for help

As we saw in Chapter 4, the Collision Regulations specify recognised distress signals but state that they should not be made unless a vessel or person is in serious and immediate danger and requiring urgent help'. The most common distress signals are a red rocket or hand flare, raising and lowering of outstretched arms, and a Mayday call on VHF, as described in Chapter 8.

If you are in need of urgent assistance but you are not 'in serious and immediate danger' you may make a Pan Pan call on VHF. The recognised visual signal is flying of the 'V' flag (white with a red St Andrew's cross).

Abandoning ship

You should only abandon ship as a last resort, if your boat is in imminent danger of sinking or, if on fire, staying aboard would endanger life. Otherwise you are more likely to be found and rescued if you stay on board. If you do decamp into a liferaft or inflatable (an acceptable alternative to a liferaft only in inshore waters and in summer) make sure it is secured to the boat by a line before putting it into the water. Put on lifejackets, if you haven't already done so, and if you have time take extra, warm clothing, some food and water, any flares that you haven't already fired, the first aid kit and seasick pills.

DINGHY DANGERS

If, when you arrive at your destination, you are moored not to a pontoon or a quayside, but to a buoy or piles (or maybe you are anchored), the most dangerous part of the passage may be yet to come: getting ashore in the dinghy.

Take great care when getting into and out of a dinghy. Step into (and from) the centreline of the boat or you may tip it up. Inflatables are more stable than rigid dinghies but they have their own foibles, like sliding away from underneath you if you apply any sideways force as you get in or out. Always sit down, and sit still, as soon as you are in the boat.

Never overload a dinghy; make several runs ashore rather than try to cram everyone in for one trip. Always arrange people—and gear—so that the boat is level and properly trimmed fore and aft. Don't be embarrassed to wear lifejackets if it's blowing hard and the water's choppy (children should always wear lifejackets in a dinghy), and don't be afraid to stay put and wait for things to calm down.

10 Know your engine

You don't have to be an all-round ace mechanic to own and operate a motor boat, but you need to know enough about the engine in your boat to be able to look after it and identify and put right the most commonly occurring faults. Even on twin-engined boats the loss of one engine can make life difficult, and it is far from inconceivable that both engines should fail, perhaps through the same problem, like dirt in the fuel, or a cooling water blockage.

It's not so much what goes on inside an engine that need concern you—though you should know the basic principles of petrol or diesel operation—as its life-support systems. It is faults in the supply of fuel, air, coolant (nearly always water in marine engines) and lubricating oil that are most likely to cause problems. Luckily these are the faults that a boat owner can most easily prevent or cure.

This chapter covers the basic principles of looking after a marine engine, but should not be a substitute for your engine manual; follow its instructions on maintenance and servicing to the letter and you will greatly reduce your chances of breakdown.

INBOARD ENGINES

Fuel supply (diesel)

In a typical diesel engine the fuel flows from the tank through a preliminary filter and water separator (usually combined), a lift pump (with filter or sediment chamber) and the main filter or filters to the injection pump. From here it is pumped at high pressure to the injectors, which deliver a carefully measured amount of fuel into the cylinder head, rejecting the rest, which is returned direct to the fuel tank.

Diesel fuel has three enemies, from which it needs to be kept apart: dirt, water and air. Take great care not to let any dirt or water into the tank when refuelling. If your tank has a sump—regrettably rare on modern boats—you should regularly drain off the dirt and water (heavier than diesel) that will inevitably collect in it. If your fuel is contaminated to the point where the filters can't cope, the tank will have to be drained and cleaned out, and this is a difficult and dirty job. Water can build up in a tank through con-

densation; the best way to combat this problem is to leave your boat with full tanks.

Filter elements should be replaced at least once a year (preferably either at the beginning or end of the season), and the sediment chambers and water separators in the filter housings should be cleaned out at the same time. As when refuelling, be very careful not to let any dirt into the system while you do it. Even the smallest specks, from an old filter via your hands for example, can cause trouble.

Air can be sucked into the fuel through joints in the line; unions may be tight enough to stop fuel getting out but not air getting in, causing your engine to lose power and maybe stop altogether.

The fuel system will need to be bled of air after you have carried out any work on it. Vent screws are provided for this purpose; taking each in turn, as instructed in the engine manual, slacken them off while pumping fuel through by hand with the lever on the lift pump, until no more bubbles of air are emerging. If you have only been working on the fuel line between the tank and the injection pump—on the filters for example—you will probably have to bleed only this part of the system, but after working on the injectors the high-pressure pipes will need bleeding as well, by slackening the injector inlet unions, and this involves turning the engine over on the starter.

Bleeding your engine is not the kind of operation you want to find yourself doing for the first time in a lumpy sea, in a panic. Familiarise yourself with the procedure by doing it when your boat is in the relative comfort of her home mooring.

Repair and servicing of fuel pumps and injectors should be left to your service agent, but a competent amateur can replace a faulty injector with a spare, taking care not to damage fuel pipes and unions.

Fuel supply (petrol)

The fuel system on a four-stroke petrol engine is similar in its early stages to a diesel system but completely different in the final method of delivery to the cylinder head. The fuel passes through a preliminary filter and water separator via the lift pump, which has a built-in filter, and on some engines

◆ Changing the fuel filter on a diesel engine, an operation which should be be carried out at least once a year if dirt in your fuel doesn't force you to do it more often. Before you fit a new filter ensure that the lip of the housing and the top of the new filter are clean.

◆ Slackening the drain tap on a preliminary fuel-cum-water separator. You should place a container underneath to catch any water (or fuel) that comes out. On a diesel installation you may need to bleed the system after draining any water off, by slackening the vent screws in the fuel line.

(generally the more powerful models) through a further filter to the carburettor. The carburettor delivers the right mixture of fuel and air through the throttle, which controls its flow, to the inlet manifold and into the cylinders.

Very fine particles of dirt are less likely to cause problems than on a diesel engine, but take the same precautions as with diesel to keep dirt and water, which can be a big problem, out of your fuel tank. Any filters that are fitted should be renewed or washed (in clean petrol) at least once a year. And it's as well to check your water separator at regular intervals through the season. If it's of the transparent kind you only have to look, and drain off any water that's there. If not, slacken the drain tap—holding a container under it—to see if it's water or petrol that comes out.

Water in the fuel is one of the most likely causes of a petrol engine losing power or stopping, but dirt can also be the culprit, blocking the jets inside the carburettor. On some simple engines it is quite possible to clean the jets yourself but on most engines the job is best left to the professionals.

The other problem with petrol, of course, is its flammability. Proper ventilation is essential; if the engine compartment isn't naturally well ventilated—and few are—it should have an extractor fan and this should always be run for a few minutes before starting up. When fuelling or doing any work on or near the engine, make sure there are no naked lights, such as a lit cigarette, nearby.

Ignition system (petrol)

Most marine petrol engines have coil ignition, identical to that on most cars, in which a high voltage is generated by the ignition coil and sent to the spark plug in each cylinder head via a distributor.

Spark plugs need regular attention. Every 50 running hours, remove them and check that they are clean and that the gap between the electrodes is what it should be. Clean them, using a stiff brush and petrol or white spirit, and adjust the gap if necessary, taking care not to damage the central electrode. Always carry a complete spare set of the correct type of plug. The contact breaker points inside the distributor also need looking at regularly, and adjusting and cleaning as necessary. If they are badly pitted they should be replaced.

Spark plugs and contact breakers are two of the things to check—along with the various kinds of fuel blockage—in the event of an engine failing or refusing to start, but if it's not even turning over look to the battery or the starter motor.

Not surprisingly, damp is one of the main causes of ignition system problems on marine petrol engines, and sometimes the cure is simply a quick rub-down of connections, plugs and points with a dry cloth, and the use of a water-repellent spray such as WD-40.

Air supply

Diesel and petrol engines burn about 15 times as much air as fuel. And like fuel, air needs to be clean. The filter on an engine air intake is less likely to clog suddenly than a fuel filter but it's one of the things to look at if an engine loses power for no obvious reason, or if you start producing black exhaust smoke. Another possibility is that the engine-room air inlet has been blocked. Air filters should be cleaned every three months or 150 engine hours, whichever comes first.

Cooling systems

The vast majority of inboard engines are water-cooled. Some of these are 'raw water' cooled, the coolant being whatever the boat is floating in, be it salt water, river water, lake water or canal water. Some are 'keel cooled' by an internal, fresh water supply that is in turn cooled by being run along pipes low down in the bilge. But most—by a long way—are cooled using both raw and fresh water. Raw water is pumped in from outside and does some cooling (usually in engine oil and gearbox oil coolers) before passing through a heat exchanger; this in turn cools an internal fresh water circuit which cools the engine block and head, and the exhaust manifold. The raw water then goes overboard, usually via the exhaust, which serves both to cool the exhaust gases and reduce exhaust noise levels.

Heat exchanger cooling, or indirect cooling as it's also known, has one significant advantage. It uses the best coolant available—the water around the boat—but avoids passing it through the engine where, especially if it's salt water, it can cause serious corrosion.

Water cooling systems, of any kind, need to be regularly checked over. With indirect or raw water cooling, check the strainer daily, and clear it of any weed or debris, and when starting up check that water is coming out with the exhaust, or from the water outlet if you have a dry exhaust. With indirect or keel cooling the level of fresh water in the header tank should also be checked daily. Every month or so you should check all the hoses and clips on the cooling system.

When under way keep an eye on the engine temperature gauge. If it rises above its normal reading shut down the engine immediately and investigate. The most likely cause in a raw water or indirect cooling system is a blocked inlet strainer. Another possibility is a damaged water pump impeller (most likely in the raw water pump if the engine has indirect cooling). On most engines the water pump is easily accessible and the impeller easily replaceable, assuming you have a spare.

If there's nothing wrong with the strainer or the pump the problem could be a fault in the thermostat,

↞ Checking the raw water strainer, which should be cleaned if it has trapped any weed or debris. Turn the seacock off before you do this and remember to turn it on again before you start the engine.

↞ A blockage in the raw water cooling circuit is likely to damage the water pump impeller. On most engines you simply unscrew the face plate and ease out the old impeller before inserting the new one, twisting it in the direction of flow as you do so. In this case the whole pump had to be removed to get at the impeller.

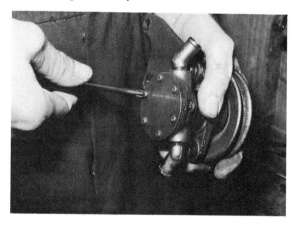

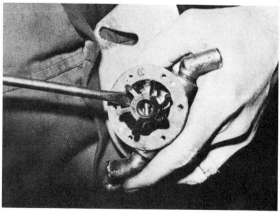

which can be replaced if you have a spare. As a temporary measure, it can be removed altogether if that is the only way to get the water flowing again. On an indirect or keel cooling system, the problem could be a loss of fresh water.

Whenever you leave your boat, close the raw water inlet seacock, remembering of course to turn it back on before starting up the engines on your next outing.

Air-cooled engines are popular on canal boats which, with raw water or indirect cooling, are vulnerable to debris. Air cooling is very simple, but such engines tend to be noisier and the large-bore trunking required for the air takes up a lot of space. If an air-cooled engine overheats it could be because the air inlet has been inadvertently covered, or because the fan belt has broken.

Lubrication

To run smoothly, all engines depend on a proper flow of the right kind of lubricating oil. In diesel and petrol inboard engines oil is held in a sump at the bottom of the engine, and is pumped through a relief valve (which controls oil pressure), a filter and the aforementioned cooler to the various moving parts of the engine. It then finds its way back to the sump by gravity. A gearbox also needs oil and has its own supply in its own sump.

The oil level in the engine should be checked on the dipstick on every outing, before starting the engine. The gearbox oil level should be checked every two or three weeks, and more frequently during heavy use. When topping up, make sure you use the specified grade of oil. Renew the oil filter elements at least once a year and change the oil at the regular intervals recommended in your engine manual.

When under way, keep an eye on your oil pressure gauge, or, if there isn't one, watch out for the warning light. Don't let the pressure fall lower than the recommended minimum (and don't let the light come on) without stopping the engine and investigating. If you don't the engine may seize up. The problem could be a blocked filter, an oil leak, a defective pump, overheating (which your temperature gauge or alarm should have indicated) or a damaged engine bearing. Or it could just be that you have allowed the oil level to drop below the minimum mark on the dipstick.

♦ **Checking the oil level. This should be a daily job when your boat is in use, along with checking the level of the freshwater coolant.**

On inboard-powered boats with conventional drives (for outdrives see the section further on) the stern gland, where the drive shaft passes out through the hull, also needs lubricating. Stern glands are lubricated either with grease or by water. If with grease give one turn of the greaser before every outing and every three or four hours during a long passage, and replenish when necessary. If by water the job is done automatically, by a feed from the engine cooling circuit. Check the stern gland, whichever type it is, before and after every trip, and every hour or so on passage. A slight drip, say two or three a minute, is acceptable. If more, the stern gland nuts might need tightening; if there's no drip and the gland is hot—too hot to touch—they might need slackening.

Electrics

Most boats have a 12V system (some larger craft work on 24V) based on lead-acid batteries, charged by alternators attached to the engine and belt-driven off the crankshaft. The usual arrangement on cruising boats is to have two batteries, one reserved for engine starting.

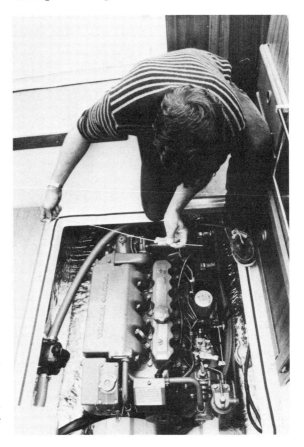

● Checking and adjusting the alternator drive belt tension—there should be half an inch (13mm) play (and no more) in the longest part of the belt.

● The drive and exhaust bellows on an outdrive-powered boat should be checked regularly for wear and replaced at least every two years.

Unless your batteries are of the maintenance-free variety, check the level of the electrolyte regularly, once a week, and top up with distilled water when necessary—the tops of the plates should be just covered. At the same time check the alternator drive belt for wear and tension—there should be no more than half an inch (13mm) of play in it. Keep the terminals of your batteries clean and lightly greased with Vaseline. Batteries will slowly discharge even when idle; charge them up at least every six weeks by running the engine, unless you have a charger of the marine, voltage-regulated type, which can safely be left connected to the mains supply.

When under way keep an eye on your ammeter or voltmeter. An ammeter should show a significant charge when you start up, and then drop—but not to a negative reading. A voltmeter should steady down at between 13V and 15V on a 12V system. If an ammeter shows a negative charge, or a voltmeter less than 12V (or if the red battery warning light should come on), something is wrong. Stop the engine and check the alternator drive belt. If an engine fails to start, and fails even to turn over, the battery or wiring must be the prime suspect, though the problem could be a faulty starter motor.

Outdrives

If your engine works through an outdrive rather than a conventional shaft drive, remember that this also needs checking and looking after. Its internal gearing is lubricated by oil just like a conventional gearbox, and needs checking and topping up. Outdrives incorporate a water intake for engine cooling, and an outlet for the exhaust, with used raw water coolant injected into it. The strainer, inside the boat, will need checking in the normal way, but in the event of overheating you should also check that the water intake on the outdrive leg has not been blocked. The rubber bellows through which the drive shaft passes into the outdrive, and the secondary, exhaust bellows should be regularly checked for wear, and replaced at least every two years.

OUTBOARD ENGINES

Fuel and lubrication

Apart from a few low-powered engines based on four-stroke petrol motors, and a few diesels, outboard engines are two-strokes that run on a mixture of petrol and oil, acting as both fuel and lubricant. The ratio of petrol to oil varies from engine to engine; usually 50:1, or 100:1, but only 25:1 in some small models. Make sure you use the right mixture and the specified grade of oil, and mix the oil and petrol properly. Many outboards, mostly the more powerful models, have 'oil injection'; the oil, held in its own reservoir, is automatically mixed with the petrol in the correct ratio, which varies with the load on the engine.

Outboards up to and including 4hp have integral fuel tanks, while more powerful models draw fuel from a separate tank. Make sure the air vent on top of the tank and the fuel cock on the engine are open before starting. With a separate tank you usually have to prime the system with a rubber hand bulb in the fuel line.

As with a four-stroke petrol inboard, dirt or water in the fuel can cause problems, and the water separator-cum-filter, where fitted (some small engines don't have them), should be regularly checked.

Ignition system

Most modern outboard engines have CD (capacitor discharge) ignition in which each spark plug has its own coil and there are no moving parts such as contact breaker points. CD ignition is inherently more reliable than coil or magneto ignition, although if it does go wrong it is beyond amateur repair. Older outboards and some small modern ones may have magneto ignition in which possible failures include damaged or worn contact breaker points, loose connections or a faulty condenser.

Spark plugs are more susceptible to fouling in two-stroke engines, particularly on those that are run for long periods at low revs, as are many outboards. Starting problems are often resolved by removing and cleaning the spark plugs, and may be avoided by giving them regular attention, as described in the section on inboard engine ignition.

Air supply

Outboards, like inboards, need a generous supply of air. The air inlets, through the hood and on the engine itself, must be kept clear and the air filter, if there is one, should be checked at least twice a season, and replaced if necessary.

Cooling system

Outboards are cooled by raw water, drawn in through an inlet in the lower unit and pumped out through an outlet near the top of the drive leg, making it easy to check that the cooling water is circulating. A blockage in the water circuit could be caused by a damaged water pump impeller (carry a spare) or a blocked water inlet.

Lower unit

The gearing in an outboard's lower unit needs lubricating with the specified oil. Regularly check the level and change the oil at the manufacturer's recommended intervals. The main danger here is contamination of the oil with water, working its way through the seals around the prop shaft, and indicated by discolouration and cloudiness. Engines left on boats afloat should be tilted up clear of the water when not in use.

To protect their gearing, outboards are built so that the propeller will slip if it should hit anything solid. On smaller outboards a shear pin through prop and shaft will break, and will need replacing (carry some spares). On larger engines a rubber bush in the hub ensures that the prop can't come to a sudden stop.

➤ Spark plugs on two-stroke outboard engines are more susceptible to fouling than on inboard engines (and the handful of four-stroke outboards). Starting problems may be caused by fouled plugs, which should be removed, using a proper plug spanner (top), and cleaned using a wire brush and petrol or white spirit (bottom). Check that the gap between the electrodes is as it should be; adjust if necessary. Your maintenance schedule should include removing, cleaning and checking your plugs every 50 running hours.

WINTER CARE

If you leave your boat afloat during the winter you can keep your engine in commission so long as you run it every two or three weeks; even if only for a few minutes. Turn the engine over several times before allowing it to fire—by not giving it any throttle and, on a diesel engine, by pulling the stop lever out—to get the oil circulating.

If you can't get down to the boat to do this, then the engine will have to be inhibited to prevent corrosion and general deterioration. It will also have to be inhibited if you take your boat out of the water for the winter. Ask your local service agent to do the job or do it yourself, following the procedure laid down in the engine manual. The essential features of inhibiting an engine are the pumping-out and replacement of the oil and the draining of the raw-water cooling circuit.

Pump out the oil, having run the engine warm, and renew the oil filter element. Refill with new oil and circulate by running the engine again for a few minutes. Use the specified grade of oil or, if the boat is to be unused for six months or more, a rust-proofing oil (which will have to be replaced at the start of the following season).

The raw-water cooling circuit should be drained and, if possible, flushed through with fresh water, then drained again, and flushed through a second time with fresh water containing a soluble rust-proofing oil, before draining once more. If the boat is afloat this operation involves turning off the seacock and disconnecting the suction pipe, to insert it into a suitable container. If the boat is out of the water you can connect a hose to the skin fitting and lead that into your container. In either case take care not to run the engine dry.

The engine air inlet should be blanked off to keep moisture out, and, if possible, the exhaust outlet should be plugged for the same reason. Spray all electrical connections with a water-repellent such as WD-40. Remove the battery or batteries and take them home, storing them somewhere protected from frost and charging them up once a month.

Outdrive legs should be washed down and the lower unit should be filled with oil, after checking that it is not contaminated with water. Remember to reduce the oil level to normal before you next run the engine.

Outboard engines should be inhibited in similar fashion to inboards, and in addition they should be washed down with fresh water and the fuel lines and carburettor should be drained. If the engine is small enough to be removed, the operation should be much easier and the engine will benefit from spending the winter under cover.

◆ Pumping out (and replacing) the lubricating oil is one of the essential features of winterising an inboard engine. Some larger engines are fitted with a permanent sump pump; for others you will need to buy or borrow a simple pump like this one if you are going to do the job yourself.

As protection from electrolytic corrosion, outboards have a zinc sacrificial anode attached to the lower unit. Check this from time to time, and when half of it has been sacrificed, replace it.

Electrics
The smallest outboards are hand-started by a recoil cord on top of the flywheel. Electric starting with some form of electrical supply is generally available as an option on outboards of between about 5hp and 40hp, and is standard on more powerful engines. In that 5hp to 40hp bracket some engines are fitted with an alternator which can supply AC current to power navigation and domestic lights; unless a rectifier is fitted it will not produce a DC current to charge a battery. Others do offer DC and it is standard on larger engines.

Installation
Outboards should be set up so that the anti-cavitation plate above the propeller is level with, or just below, the bottom of the transom. Boats with a transom height (the vertical distance from the outer lip of the engine well to the bottom of the transom) of more than about 20in (0.5m) will need a long-shaft outboard.

Engines of up to 20hp can be clamped to the transom, with a safety line securing the engine to the boat in case the clamps should work loose. More powerful engines should be through-bolted, after they have been set up at the right height. Engines of up to 40hp may be tiller-steered or rigged with remote steering; over 40hp and remote steering is essential. All moving parts of the controls and tilt mechanism should be clean and lightly greased.

Besides being set at the right height, outboards need to be trimmed to the optimum angle, either by moving the pin in the mounting bracket or by working the power trim fitted to more powerful models (see the section in Chapter 9 on adjusting trim for different sea conditions). The larger outboards have a small trim tab under the cavitation plate which can be adjusted to counteract the effect of propeller torque.

➤ **An outboard engine should usually be installed so that the anti-cavitation plate is level with or just below the bottom of the boat's transom. This engine has been mounted a little too high.**

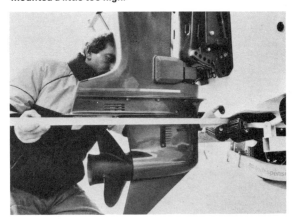

PROPELLERS

Pitch

Diameter

When you buy a boat, new or secondhand, the propeller(s) should be the optimum size, matched to engine power, shaft rpm (less than engine rpm if you have a reduction gearbox) and hull design. Size is expressed in diameter and pitch. Pitch is the distance the prop would move during one revolution if it didn't slip. In practice propellers slip by between 15%, on fast powerboats, to 50% on heavy displacement craft.

The mind-boggling formulae devised to calculate prop size suggest that selection is an exact science, but as often as not it's a matter of trial and error, and generalisations: the larger the diameter, the more efficient the prop; for better low-speed thrust increase diameter, reduce pitch; for more speed (but less acceleration and economy) increase pitch, reduce diameter; engine not reaching proper rpm = diameter and/or pitch too large; engine over-revving = diameter and/or pitch too small.

11 Boat care and maintenance

Whatever claims boatbuilders make for the low-maintenance qualities of glassfibre (which these days accounts for over 95 per cent of motor boat production), boats still require regular attention to fight the ravages of a hostile environment. Glassfibre may need less maintenance than wood but on most boats there's a lot else that water and a water-laden atmosphere can corrode, rot, tarnish or turn mouldy.

That paints a rather gloomy picture of boating, but many owners actually relish the time they have to spend working on their boats. And even if, like most people, you see maintenance as a necessary chore, it does have its rewards. A smart boat is a boat you can take pride in. A boat in good repair is a boat you can take to sea—or down the river or along the canal or across the lake—with confidence.

It's tempting, if you can afford it, to pay someone else to do the worst of the work, but the benefits of doing as much as possible yourself are more than financial. Spend a day down in the bilges checking the seacocks and you will be better equipped to carry out emergency repairs should one of them fail during your summer cruise.

● **To keep a glassfibre boat's topsides and upperworks in good condition polish them at least once a year, using a non-silicone polish.**

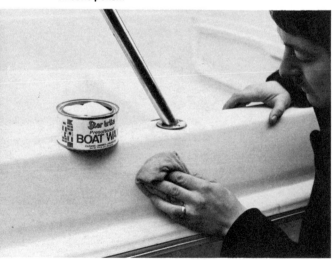

The best way of coping with the workload is not to leave everything until the traditional pre-season fitting-out period, but to spread as much as possible of the work throughout the year; also to be systematic, keeping a record of the work to be done and the work you have done.

Engine maintenance was covered in Chapter 10. Here we will look at the rest of the boat, starting with...

HULL AND DECK

Cleaning

To keep a glassfibre boat in good condition you should wash down the topsides, deck and super-structure at least twice a year with a mild detergent in warm water. Obstinate grease marks and rust stains can be removed with a glassfibre cleaner and to help keep all these surfaces clean, polish them at least once a year using a non-silicone polish.

After every trip out to sea rinse down your deck and topsides, and the windows and deck fittings, with fresh water.

Minor repairs

Keep a constant look-out for damage to the surface gelcoat of a glassfibre hull or deck. You may be able to eliminate small surface scratches or scores using a rubbing compound or fine wet-and-dry sandpaper and polish. Deeper cracks or scores can be repaired using an epoxy filler. With a chisel, slightly enlarge the damaged area and make a dovetail of it by under-cutting the edges. Wash out the cavity with acetone, allow to dry and then apply the filler, using enough to leave it slightly proud of the surrounding surface. Cover the whole area with cellophane, taped down around the edges, and allow 24 hours for the filler to cure. Then rub down with wet-and-dry sandpaper and polish.

Whenever your boat is out of the water inspect the undersides for blisters. They may be harmless—such as blisters in the anti-fouling with the gelcoat underneath undamaged. But they may, if you are unlucky, be symptoms of osmosis, in which water has permeated under the gelcoat into voids in the laminate, reacted with chemicals in the laminate to form a chemical solution and then (by the chemical process which gives the dreaded hull disease its name) sucked more water through. The blisters are bulges in the gelcoat where this has happened. Pierce each blister and, if it is osmotic, you will notice the distinctive vinegary smell of the solution that spurts out. Carefully remove the blister and you will see the glass laminate underneath.

If a thorough inspection reveals only a handful of small blisters, with no visible damage to the laminate, you could cure the problem yourself, repairing each blister by the method just described for repairing surface cracks. But it's advisable to seek professional advice. If the hull is badly affected you may have to employ a boatyard, perhaps one of the those specialising in osmosis treatment, to carry out the difficult (and expensive) job of stripping off the gelcoat and building up a replacement with layers of epoxy.

You can use epoxy fillers to repair minor gouges in wooden and metal hulls as well. The kind of weaknesses likely to be suffered by wooden hulls are loose caulking, damaged fastenings—look for damaged or missing dowels—and rot, which if suspected can be checked by poking the plank concerned with a sharp spike to see if it is soft. Unless you are a competent amateur shipwright you will need professional help to put any of these problems right. On steel hulls look for rust on any areas exposed by damage to the paintwork. Chip and wire-brush it off before touching up the paintwork.

Painting

To owners of glassfibre boats, hull painting means anti-fouling the bottom. That said, the painting of topsides and decks is becoming more and more common as a cure for the lacklustre look that many boats suffer from after ten years or so.

When anti-fouling, as when applying any kind of paint, follow the paintmaker's instructions to the letter. Remember that even the new tin-free brands of anti-fouling are poisonous, so take care when washing down the dissolving types and particular care when removing the 'hard' types. Always wear a face mask, and never use a disc sander. Most anti-foulings are not suitable for aluminium alloy surfaces, such as outboard or outdrive legs.

First-time painting of glassfibre topsides or deck requires careful and time-consuming preparation. They must be cleansed of any polish or remaining mould release agent, using a special cleaner, and then sanded to provide a key for the primer. Study the manufacturers' literature on suitable paints. As the main reason for doing the job is to restore the original, glossy appearance of the boat you may prefer to pay a boatyard—one used to painting glassfibre boats—to do the work for you.

Wooden boats look best if rubbed down and given a new topcoat every year, but with modern paints and careful use they can go unpainted for two or three years. Every five to ten years, depending on the condition of the wood and the underlying paint, all the paintwork will have to be stripped off for a complete repaint.

Steel boats require rather different treatment. Damaged paintwork should be touched up after careful preparation (including the removal of rust if the damage has penetrated through to bare steel), but you should not build up the coating by simply slapping on new layers of paint over old. And it shouldn't be necessary; with modern epoxy paint systems on a well-prepared surface, steel hulls should not need repainting for about ten years, but then they should be repainted from bare metal.

UNDERWATER FITTINGS

Metal fittings on the bottom of a boat are vulnerable to electrolytic corrosion, especially in salt water. The water is an effective electrolyte in an electrical cell, in which metal fittings of dissimilar electro-potential are the terminals. The baser metal—the one lower down the electro-potential or 'galvanic' table—acts

➡ **Pre-season anti-fouling. Remember to wear a face mask when removing the old anti-fouling, since even the new tin-free brands are toxic.**

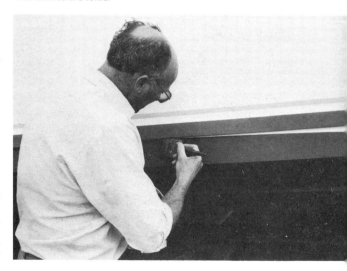

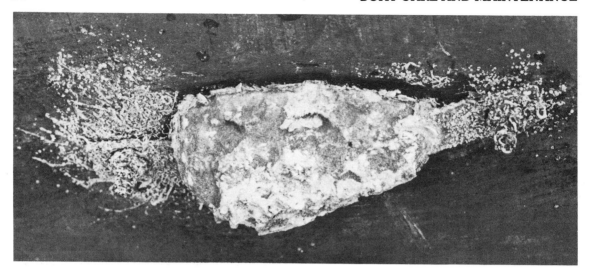

as the anode and is slowly eaten away. To prevent this potentially fatal sequence of events you need to install what is known as cathodic protection. A sacrificial anode, usually zinc, which comes very low down in the galvanic table, is bolted to the hull, turning all the other underwater metals into uncorroding cathodes. To be effective the zinc needs to be wired, inside the hull, to the fittings it is protecting.

Sacrificial anodes need to be replaced when they are more than 50 per cent wasted. For convenience they should be of a size that will need replacing once a year, when the boat comes out of the water for the winter (or for anti-fouling for the summer), at which time all the other underwater fittings should be looked at to check that the anode has been doing its job properly. If there are any signs of corrosion elsewhere, check the connecting wiring.

DECK FITTINGS

Cleats, guardrail stanchions and other attachments to the deck should be regularly checked, to see if they are still firmly attached. If there's any play it could be that a screw or nut has come loose or that the surface underneath is damaged (on glassfibre boats, fittings should be screwed or bolted through the deck into, or through, a timber backing pad).

Keep everything clean and, where appropriate, polished. Rust marks can be removed with a metal cleaner, but ask yourself why a fitting is rusting; is it attached with a screw of incompatible metal? Electrical deck connections need particular attention. A smearing of silicone grease is one of the best forms of protection.

◆ **A well-sacrificed zinc sacrificial anode. When half the anode has been wasted it is time to replace it, ensuring that it is wired to all underwater metal fittings.**

Exterior woodwork, and any paint or varnish covering it, is particularly vulnerable to deterioration. That's why teak is so popular; it can be maintained and made to look good without paint or varnish, simply by scrubbing (not sanding down) and treating with teak oil.

◆ **Regularly check, and if necessary tighten, screwed-down deck fittings such as cleats and fairleads. If any screws won't tighten, the surface underneath (and wooden backing pad on glassfibre boats) may be damaged.**

◆ A badly corroded anchor chain, well overdue for replacement. Remember that a snapped anchor chain could cost you your boat.

◆ Check the toilet seacocks and hoses at least once a year. All seacocks should be dismantled periodically—ideally every year—and checked and greased.

Anchor cable, whether chain or chain and warp, should be checked regularly, for signs of wear in the chain links or chafe in a warp. And while you have it laid out on deck for the purpose, check the lashing that should connect the bitter (inboard) end of the anchor cable to the boat (for easy letting go if you have to abandon your anchor and cable in an emergency). If you have an anchor windlass follow the maker's instructions on greasing and lubrication. Check your mooring warps too, for chafe and for fraying at the ends. The ends of most synthetic ropes can be protected by binding them with waterproof tape and fusing the tips with a lighted match, but the traditional—and still the best—way is to use a whipping.

INTERIOR

Bilges, the repository of much of the muck that is generated on a boat, as well as any water that finds its way in, should be cleaned out at least twice a year. For the best effect use one of the proprietary bilge cleaners, which will emulsify any oil in the water. If you can do the job at sea the motion of the boat will help the cleaner do its work, and you can pump out the resulting mixture into the sea, unless it is particularly oily, in which case pump out into a container that can then be disposed of in an approved tip. Either way, this is also an opportunity to test your bilge pumps. If your bilges are prone to oil contamination you could use one of the oil-absorbent mats

that many chandlers stock, although perhaps you should also do something about finding and curing the cause of the contamination.

Another messy business is the maintenance of sea toilets. Inspect the piping and its connections at least once a year, and every two or three years replace all the gaskets, diaphragms and hose clips. The toilet seacocks and any others should periodically be dismantled, checked and greased, ideally once a year, but every two or three years should be sufficient. The best way to maintain seacocks at other times is to work them, say, once a month (assuming they aren't regularly turned on and off in the normal course of events).

If you have gas on board, check the pipes and connections for wear and replace if suspect. In the event of a leak or suspected leak you can test the pipe with soapy water—escaping gas will make it bubble. Gas bottles should be in a locker, on deck or in the cockpit, with an overboard drain in the bottom; periodically check that the drain isn't blocked. Always turn the gas off at the bottle when not in use.

Steering gear should be checked for wear during the winter and at least once during the season, and greased and lubricated as necessary.

Interior woodwork should not require heavy maintenance so long as the accommodation is well ventilated and reasonably dry. Varnish should last well unless it is exposed to sunlight. Unpainted wood should be treated with a preservative.

Keep the interior of your boat well ventilated and dry, and you will avoid problems such as flaking varnish, mouldy upholstery and general deterioration. A well-designed, well-built boat will have permanent deck-head ventilators in all cabins. If yours doesn't you should somehow ensure a flow of air through the boat when you are not on board. Fix things so that you can, with reasonable security, leave a hatch slightly open at one end and a window at the other, with doors between left open. Install one or two chemical dehumidifiers (replacing the crystals when necessary) or, if you keep your boat in a marina with shore power, a mains-operated dehumidifier or a low-wattage tubular heater.

LAYING UP

Whether a boat is hauled out for the winter or left in the water, to come out for a new coat of anti-fouling in the spring, you should keep her dry, as just described. Damp is the worst enemy of a boat during the winter months. If you have a canopy, support it so that air can get in and out at both ends.

Unless you are keeping your boat in commission, remove all loose upholstery and store it somewhere dry at home. Also, take as many portable items of equipment home as is practicable, especially any expensive navigation aids. Not only will they be safer, but they too will benefit from being kept dry.

Fresh water tanks should be emptied and water systems flushed through before being drained to be left empty. Water tanks should be thoroughly cleaned every year, perhaps with one of the special water tank cleaning products. Toilets should be treated with disinfectant and, a day or two later if possible, pumped dry.

Liferafts should be delivered to the nearest service agents; the end of the season is also the best time to deal with any other items that need servicing or repairing.

If the boat comes out of the water for the winter don't delay in checking all the underwater fittings, not just for electrolytic corrosion, as already described, but for other types of wear and damage, particularly to sterngear. If propeller, shaft, shaft bracket or rudder fittings need attention you can get them seen to before the pre-summer rush. That is one of the advantages of laying up ashore. Check the general condition of the hull too. Look for those tell-tale blisters, which could mean osmosis, though a boat that is taken out of the water for the winter is less likely to suffer. That's another advantage of laying up ashore.

FITTING OUT

Anti-fouling, and other painting jobs, have already been mentioned. They are the obvious pre-summer chores, but there are other things to do before you can set off on your first outing of the season. If you have not had the boat out of the water for the winter you will need to carry out all those underwater checks, as described earlier, when you dry out or haul out to anti-foul.

Return all the furnishings and equipment you took home with you for the winter, and recover the liferaft and any equipment that you sent away for servicing or repair. Flush out and refill water tanks and recommission the toilet. Check that your flares and fire extinguishers are still in date and replace them if they are not.

Before your first trip check that all the fittings are secure and that all items of equipment are working properly.

12 Trailer boating

By keeping your boat on a trailer you gain several advantages over those who keep their boats afloat. You can vary your cruising ground at will. You can save money by not having to pay mooring fees. And if you have space to park your boat at home she is handily placed for working on during free evenings and weekends.

But there is one distinct and obvious disadvantage. The size of boat you can tow behind a car is limited, by law and by the practicalities of trailing with reasonable ease. In the UK at least, the law is quite generous about the size of boat that you can tow (see 'Trailing within the law' panel, overleaf), but towing, launching and recovering a boat of more than about 20ft (6m) can be very hard work and is really only practical for occasional trailing, say if you just launch and recover at the beginning and end of the season.

CHOOSING A TRAILER

The first requirement of a trailer is that it should have a carrying capacity to match the weight of your boat, taking into account engine and equipment. But just as important is the design of the trailer, which must support your boat in a way that spreads the load as evenly as possible. If your boat is a standard design the builder or dealer you bought her from should be able to advise you on suitable sizes and types of trailer, as will a reputable trailer dealer.

Trailers come in varying degrees of sophistication. Boat supports vary from a couple of longitudinal solid, cushion-topped rails to multiple, swivelling, rubber rollers, which a boat can be moved on to and off

➤ **By using a break-back trailer, this small cruiser can be launched from a shallow-sloping slipway without dunking the wheel hubs and risking damage to the bearings.**

more easily. All but the smallest trailers are fitted with a winch and wire for hauling a boat on. Many trailers are designed with further aids to launching and recovery. On 'break-back' trailers the frame is hinged so that the whole back part of the trailer can be tilted. A more recent development is the provision of a cross-member at the back, holding a group of rollers, which tilts in such a way that the rollers support the bow of the boat as it slides off, or is brought back on.

Your trailer should be fitted with brakes, unless your boat is light enough, and your car heavy enough, to exempt you (see 'Trailing within the law' panel). In the UK braked trailers manufactured since October 1982 must have 'hydraulically damped overrun' couplings that activate the brakes automatically, and by the appropriate amount, as the towing vehicle is slowed down by its own brakes. In its standard version the brake has to be disconnected when you want to reverse, but more and more trailers are being fitted with 'auto-reverse' brakes, which don't have to be disconnected. 'Auto-reverse' brakes will be mandatory on new, braked trailers from April 1989.

Two-wheel trailers are fine for boats of up to about three-quarters of a ton, but most trailers with carrying capacities greater than that have four wheels. Four-wheelers are considerably heavier, so increasing the total weight of your load, but they do offer the safety factor of a back-up tyre on each side in the event of a puncture. On the subject of tyres, do carry

▲ **This sophisticated trailer has a tilting rear cross member with its own set of rollers, enabling the boat to be launched easily and keeping the wheel hubs dry.**

a spare one for your trailer, whether it's a two-wheeler or a four-wheeler, as well as a jack and wheel brace; those designed for your car probably won't work on the trailer.

INSURANCE

Make sure that boat and trailer are properly insured. Third party insurance (at least) on your trailer should be included in your vehicle insurance, together with third party cover for your boat while she is in transit. Your boat's policy should provide cover for the boat, excluding third party, while in transit, and full cover once the boat is detached from the car. Theft and damage cover for your trailer should be included either in your vehicle or boat insurance. Check that it's covered while detached from your car.

SUITABLE CARS

The weight of your car is as important as its power. The weight of your trailer and its load should not exceed the car manufacturer's stated towing weight limit, which is usually not very different from the car's own weight. Car manufacturers also specify a maximum trailer nose weight—the weight of the coupling on the tow ball fitted to the car—and this should not be exceeded either. It's usually somewhere between 90lb and 165lb (40kg to 75kg). You do of course have some control over the nose weight, by adjusting the position of the boat on the trailer, or any equipment that is in the boat.

Most boats up to about 18ft (5.5m) can be trailed quite adequately behind 1600cc family saloons, though more power will be useful, particularly for towing to hilly areas. Boats of 18ft to 20ft (5.5–6m) will require more power and for anything over 20ft you will need a large saloon car—preferably with one of the more powerful engine options—or a four-wheel drive vehicle. These offer a clear advantage with larger loads, especially on steep slipways.

ON THE ROAD

Unless you drive articulated lorries for a living your first experience of towing a boat can be quite alarming. Suddenly you are driving something more than twice as long as you are used to, the rear part of which may at times head in a different direction from the one you are steering. Towing a trailer demands the learning of several new driving techniques.

When turning, allow for your greater length and for the trailer's tendency to cut corners. Forget this and the trailer could mount the kerb—and hit anyone standing close to it. If you take a corner too fast the opposite can happen; the trailer's momentum can cause it to swing outwards and clip another vehicle.

When reversing, remember that the trailer will turn in the opposite direction to the car. When reversing round a corner, always start off with car and trailer in line, then begin the manoeuvre by applying the 'wrong' lock to get the trailer turning in the desired direction, but not to the degree where it 'jack-knifes'.

When going downhill, apply as little brake as possible; slow down by changing down to a low gear.

One of the most alarming things that can happen when towing is 'snaking', when the trailer starts to weave from side to side. Avoid the natural panic reaction of slamming on your brakes; it will probably make things worse. You can do nothing other than ease your foot off the accelerator and slow down gently. Prevention is better than cure; snaking is usually caused by driving too fast, especially when going downhill, but it can be brought on by poor weight distribution or uneven tyre pressures. Strong side winds can also start a trailer snaking, and so can the buffeting you get when being passed by a high-sided vehicle; in both circumstances slowing down, preferably before you start to snake, is the answer.

If boat and trailer start to pitch the cause could be poor fore-and-aft weight distribution, or defective suspension—either the trailer's or the car's.

Besides driving carefully you should also, before you set out, make sure that your boat is properly

secured to the trailer. Use at least two broad web-bing straps, with tensioners. Pass them over the boat and clear of any fittings that might give under the pressure. Finally, remember that the weight of the trailer will probably mean you have to make adjustments to your car's headlights and mirrors, and follow the manufacturer's instructions on tyre pressures when trailing.

LAUNCH AND RECOVERY

The golden rule of launching is not to do so immedi-ately on arriving at your destination. If your trailer's wheels are immersed while they are still hot the bearings can suffer serious damage, especially in salt water. The air inside the hub will cool rapidly on contact with the water and the resulting vacuum will draw in water through the seals.

Wait for at least half an hour, preferably longer, before launching, and even then try to avoid immers-ing the wheel hubs if you can. Whether this is possible will depend on the slope of the slipway—it is difficult to avoid on a shallow-angled slip—and whether or not you have a break-back or swivel-beam trailer. Reverse the trailer down to a point where the boat will float, and from where she can be pushed off without an uncomfortable drop into the water. For a controlled launch, attach the winch wire and ease it out as the boat goes.

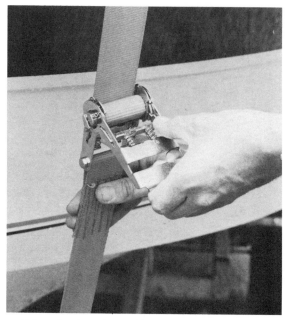

← Using a tensioner in a webbing strap to ensure the strap is holding the boat down securely. Make sure the tensioner is well away from any vulnerable surface it might damage when the webbing strap flaps or vibrates.

← Sometimes it is impossible to launch or recover a boat without immersing the trailer wheel hubs, at least with a conventional trailer. Always wait for an hour or more after arriving before you launch to allow the wheels to cool, and if you have to dunk the hubs they should be checked and greased before you drive away.

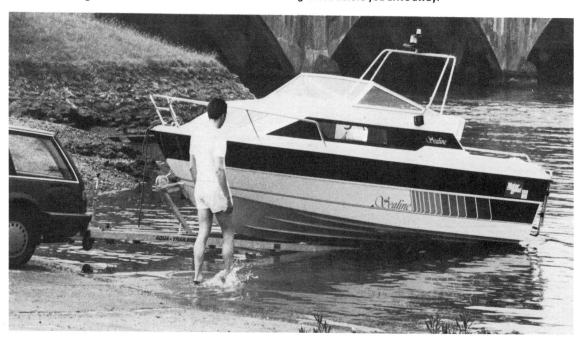

When recovering, back the trailer to the point where you can easily lift the bow on to it, which will probably be rather further into the water than when launching. Make sure the boat is properly lined up with the trailer before you start hauling, and guide her into the right position as she comes out of the water. Be precise and it will be a lot easier; what's more you won't have the awkward and potentially back-breaking job of moving the boat about when she's up on the trailer.

When planning any kind of boat-trailing trip, find out what you can about the slipways in the area you are visiting. The mere mention of a slipway in a local guide or pilot book doesn't even guarantee its existence, let alone vouch for its suitability for a boat and trailer of any weight or size. *Where to launch your boat*, published by Barnacle Marine, lists hundreds of slipways in Britain, with useful information such as tidal restrictions (if any) and availability of car and trailer parking. If you are in doubt make local enquiries, or better still do a reconnaissance yourself, by car alone.

↞ When the boat is on the trailer, projections such as outboard engine propellers must by law be covered by some form of protection (see overleaf).

TRAILER MAINTENANCE

Trailers need to be maintained, like the boats that sit on them. Wheels should be the principal object of attention. The condition and pressure of the tyres should be checked as regularly as those on your car; their condition is subject to the same strict regulations that govern car tyres. Wheel bearings should be checked and greased every three months, and after every trip when you have had to dunk the wheels up to hub level while launching or recovering.

The moving parts of the coupling and the jockey wheel (the little adjustable-height wheel that supports the front of the trailer when detached from the car) should also be kept well greased. Your trailer manual should tell you what else needs doing. Not for the first time in this book the advice is 'Follow the manufacturer's instructions'.

TRAILING WITHIN THE LAW

When towing a boat you must conform to the legal requirements affecting the size and weight of car and load, the type of trailer you use and its fittings, the way a boat is secured to the trailer, and the speed at which you can drive. Stick within the law, not only to avoid the risk of prosecution (traffic police are noted for their attention to car trailers and trailer loads) but for your own safety as well.

The following is a summary of the relevant trailing regulations in force in the UK, as they apply to trailers and boats:

Size limits (metres first, as they are what the law deals in). The maximum length of a trailer, assuming it's a conventional trailer towed by any vehicle (including a Land Rover) less than a 'heavy motor vehicle' is 7m (23ft 0in), excluding the length of the drawbar with which it is attached to the car. The maximum width of a trailer is 2.3m (7ft 6in). The length of your boat may be longer than 7m but if the stern overhangs by more than 1m (3ft 3in) the light board (see below) must be positioned on the boat so that it is no more than 1m from the stern, and still clearly visible. Beam should not exceed 2.9m (9ft 6in).

Brakes Trailers without brakes are only permitted if the total weight of the trailer and load (boat, engine and equipment) does not exceed 750kg (1650lb) and if the weight of the towing vehicle is at least twice that of the trailer and load. From April 1989 all new braked trailers must have auto-reverse brakes.

Braked trailers should be fitted with an emergency braking device, which will stop the trailer should it become uncoupled. On single-axle trailers with a gross weight (trailer and boat) not exceeding 1500kg (3300lb) a safety chain, capable of holding the front of the trailer off the road in the event of an uncoupling, is an acceptable alternative. Braked trailers should also be fitted with a parking brake, capable of holding the trailer and load on gradients of up to 18% (1 in 5½).

Lights, reflectors and number plates
Trailers should carry a number plate showing the number of the towing vehicle, plus the following lights and reflectors (usually all together on a board, the lights connected through a socket on the back of the car and working with the equivalent lights on the car): red tail lights, brake lights, direction indicators, number plate light, one or two fog lamps (unless the trailer was manufactured before October 1979 and first used before April 1980), and red triangular reflectors. In addition, trailers over 1.6m (5ft 3in) wide (all but the smallest boat trailers) should have two white front marker lights, and trailers over 5m (16ft 5in) long should have two orange reflectors on each side. Fitting front marker lights on to boat trailers can be a problem but it seems to be acceptable to mount them on the front of the board, on the outer edges where they can be clearly seen.

Mirrors In addition to the interior and offside mirrors mandatory on all cars, a nearside mirror must also be fitted if the trailer and its load obscures the view in the interior mirror (which it nearly always will).

Safety of load The boat must be securely held on the trailer and there must be no sharp edges or projections that could be dangerous to other vehicles or pedestrians. Many boat trailing drivers have been prosecuted because the lower units of their outboard engines or outdrives have been deemed to be dangerous projections. A heavy-duty PVC bag, or plastic bucket or box, seem to be acceptable forms of protection.

Driving restrictions On motorways and dual carriageways the maximum speed for a car towing a trailer is 60mph; on other roads it is 50mph. You may not use the outside, overtaking lane on three-lane motorways.

Before towing overseas find out about the regulations in force in the countries you will be visiting. UK regulations on trailer construction and fittings conform to Common Market standards, but most European countries have stricter load width limits, commonly 2.5m (8ft 2in), but only 2.3m (7ft 6in) in Switzerland (for two-wheel drive cars). Make sure that car, boat and trailer are included on your insurance documents (see under 'Insurance') or the Green Card you need to carry in most European countries.

Index

* denotes illustration. Chapter subjects indicated in **bold type**